Lasting Contribution

HOW TO THINK, PLAN, AND ACT TO ACCOMPLISH MEANINGFUL WORK

Tad Waddington

A B2 Book

AGATE

CHICAGO

Printed in the United States of America.

Library of Congress Cataloging-in-Publication Data

Waddington, Tad.
  Lasting contribution : how to think, plan, and act to accomplish meaningful work / Tad Waddington.
      p. cm.
  Includes bibliographical references and index.
  ISBN-13: 978-1-932841-29-9 (pbk. : alk. paper)
  ISBN-10: 1-932841-29-6 (pbk. : alk. paper)
  1. Meaning (Philosophy) 2. Conduct of life. I. Title. II. Title: How to think, plan, and act to accomplish meaningful work.
  B105.M4W33 2007
  128'.4--dc22

                          2007015761

10   9   8   7   6   5   4   3   2

B2 Books is an imprint of Agate Publishing, Inc. Agate books are available in bulk at discount prices. For more information, go to agatepublishing.com.

Table of Contents

For Elias

I

Getting Started
THINKING CAUSALLY

The greatest use of life is to spend it for something that will outlast it.

—WILLIAM JAMES

Sooner or later every thinking person asks the immortal question: have I made a difference in the world? If you ask this question later in life, your next step is an exercise in ethical accounting: you once spilled tea on your friend's new shirt, but made up for it by saving his life after he was in a car wreck. If, however, you ask this question sooner, then your next question is: how do I make a difference? Actually that shouldn't be your next question, because it is easy to make a *difference*. A single match can burn down a forest and what a difference that makes. A better question is: how can I contribute to the world?

There are many answers to this question. You can run errands for your elderly neighbor, pick up litter in the park, or leave a generous tip for your footsore waiter. But while these activities are important, they point to the limits of the question. Imagine that cars always speed near a certain playground, and it's only a matter of time before a child is killed. You could make the world a better place if you were to stand by the road and wave a flag at the speeding cars to encourage them to slow down, but your contribution would stop the moment you stopped waving the flag. Or you could post a sign that says, "Slow." For this to be a contribution, however, drivers would have to read and heed the sign. The sign is ineffective, because the speeders might be driving too fast to see it. So you decide to change the nature of the equation. You get a speed bump installed. The speeders slow down, and the kids are safer.

So the question isn't just: how do you contribute? The question is: how do you make a contribution that lasts? Unfortunately the solutions to most of the world's problems aren't as easy as installing the occasional speed bump, so the question becomes: given that the world is big and complex, how do you make a lasting contribution? In other words, how do you accomplish something that matters? How do people like you and me achieve not the ephemeral, but the enduring; not the trivial, but the significant? The answer is that just like everything else in the world—from tea stains to speed bumps—lasting contributions *are caused*. Simply put, you *cause* a lasting contribution to happen. The problem is that the way people usually think about causality does not serve them well when it comes to thinking about taking action.

People tend to think of causality as one billiard ball striking another that ricochets into another and another. On a wintry mountain a squirrel drops an acorn. It falls and dislodges some snow. The snow slides, knocking free yet more snow, causing an avalanche. The distant roar of the avalanche startles you as you pour tea. It spills on your friend's new shirt. You apologize to your friend, but in a sense, it was the squirrel that caused the tea stain.

But even if the world does work this way, this may not be the best way to *think about* taking meaningful action. Suppose you want to help people by healing them. You plan to use your existing skills and knowledge to attend medical school to become a doctor. This thought raises some problems with our notion of billiard-ball causality: healing people, which started the whole chain of events, hasn't happened yet. Does this mean the future causes the past? Probably not. Maybe it is your *desire* to help people that starts the chain of events. But is your desire caused or is it free will? Aren't your existing skills and knowledge, your passion to contribute to the world, and your plan of going to medical school all part of the *cause* of your becoming a doctor?

When it comes to human action, skills, passions, and plans are part of causality. Some 2,300 years ago, Aristotle argued that it is useful to think in terms of four causes:

1. *Of what* a thing is made, also called the **material cause**. Clay is the material cause of a brick. Steel, rubber, and plastic are part of the material cause of a car.
2. *How* something is made, also called the **efficient cause**. The efficient cause is billiard-ball causality, the action that brings something into being. It is the gathering and firing of clay to make a brick. The workers on an assembly line are the efficient cause of a car.
3. *What* a thing is, also called the **formal cause**. The formal cause is the essence, idea, or plan of a thing.

The essence of a brick is that it is an expression of an idea of the right size, shape, and strength of an object needed for building. The engineer's design is the formal cause of a car.

4. *Why* a thing is, the sake for which a thing is done, also called the **final cause**. The final cause of a brick is to make a wall. The final cause of a car is that it helps you get from here to there.

What is the cause of climbing a mountain? The material cause is your climbing gear—oxygen, ice axes, and tents. The efficient cause is putting one foot in front of the other. The formal cause is the route you plan to take. The final cause, explained British mountaineer George Mallory, who died on Everest, is "because it is there."

Bricks, cars, and mountains, however, are simple. How do the four causes work in a complex, dynamic, and messy world such as the one in which we live? The intent of this book is to help you make a lasting contribution to the world, because when doers think before acting and when thinkers take action, remarkable results follow. When doers don't think before acting and when thinkers don't act, good people's efforts fail to achieve their full impact. It is not that that doers are stupid or that thinkers are lazy; they merely lack a theory to guide and facilitate their actions. Using Aristotle's four causes to guide and facilitate your actions can help you to think more clearly and act more effectively, which will help you to achieve lasting results— results that are worth achieving.

At this point, you may be concerned that you are not

talented enough to make a lasting contribution. In the course of this book, I will show that this concern is chimerical, but for now, here is an example of the sort of lasting contribution that is within your reach. It comes from Peter F. Drucker's book, *The Effective Executive*:

> A new hospital administrator, holding his first staff meeting, thought that a rather difficult matter had been settled to everyone's satisfaction, when one of the participants suddenly asked: "Would this have satisfied Nurse Bryan?" At once the argument started all over and did not subside until a new and much more ambitious solution to the problem had been hammered out.
>
> Nurse Bryan, the administrator learned, had been a long-serving nurse at the hospital. She was not particularly distinguished, had not in fact ever been a supervisor. But whenever a decision on patient care came up on her floor, Nurse Bryan would ask, "Are we doing the best we can do to help this patient?" Patients on Nurse Bryan's floor did better and recovered faster. Gradually over the years, the whole hospital had learned to adopt what came to be known as "Nurse Bryan's Rule"; had learned, in other words, to ask: "Are we really making the best contribution to the purpose of this hospital?"
>
> Though Nurse Bryan herself had retired almost ten years earlier, the standards she had set still made demands on people who in terms of training and position were her superiors.

Every person is capable of accomplishing as much as Nurse Bryan.

Finally, a word of warning. You will be disappointed if you believe that contribution is a nail, and this book a hammer. The world and what you must do in it to make a lasting contribution are far too complex for such a simple perspective to be effective. This book was written to help you not in the way a hammer helps you to build a house, but in the way a blueprint does. It prepares you for action.

II

Dealing With Complexity
EFFICIENT CAUSE

For every complex problem there is a solution that is simple, straightforward, and wrong.

—H. L. MENCKEN

Efficient causation is about taking action. Sometimes you can "just do it," knock down the first domino—which topples the next in a long line of dominoes—and achieve the result you want. More often, however, the world is not domino-simple. The poet Percy Bysshe Shelley nailed the nature of the problem: "Nothing in the world is single, All things...In one another's being mingle...." Business strategist Peter Senge has expressed the same idea less poetically but more precisely: "human endeavors are...systems. They...are bound by invisible fabrics of interrelated actions, which often take years to fully play out their effects on each other." Senge said this is a problem of *dynamic complexity,* which he defined as "situations where cause and effect are subtle, and where the effects over time of interventions are not obvious."

At the simplest level, dynamic complexity is the problem of the hotel shower with a delay between the faucet and water temperature, resulting in water that lunges between freezing and scalding. At more complex levels, it is the problem of the well-intentioned action that has disastrous unintended consequences, such as early settlers importing rabbits to make Australia look more like England—rabbits that ultimately caused widespread habitat destruction.

The world is not only a dynamic system; it is an *open* dynamic system. This means that it is not only complex, but also that new things can enter the picture to change the nature of the equation. For example, complex though it was, the ocean ecosystem off the shores of Peru was functioning harmoniously until an outside force intervened. In the 1950s, enterprising fishermen decided to make some easy money by harvesting 14 million tons of anchovies to sell as food for cattle and pets. Unfortunately, the guanay (a seabird) eats anchovies, and the guanays' droppings make an excellent fertilizer, particularly for plankton. Plankton feed not only the anchovies but also tuna and sea bass. After the giant Peruvian anchovy harvest, the guanay population dropped by 98.5 percent. As a result, the populations of plankton and the fish that fed on them also crashed. Now, fifty years later, the fish populations in the area have yet to recover. With one ill-conceived action, the fishermen destroyed generations of livelihood for future fishing families.

Senge suggested that the best way to deal with complex systems is with systems thinking: "Systems thinking is a discipline for seeing wholes. It is a framework for seeing interrelationships rather than things, for seeing patterns of change rather than static 'snapshots.'" He went on to say, "Seeing only individual actions and missing the structure underlying the actions...lies at the root of our powerlessness in complex situations."

Ah, but *how* do you deal with such complexities? Every situation is different so you need to engage in *considered action,* features of which include:

Acting complexly

In *The Logic of Failure,* German psychologist Dietrich Dörner summarized experiments on how people deal with complex systems. Dörner created a computer model of an imaginary country in West Africa that he called Tanaland. The people of this imaginary land depend on growing crops, gathering fruit, and herding sheep and cattle. Participants in Dörner's experiment were given the opportunity to control certain variables of the Tanaland computer model, such as whether to use irrigation and fertilizer. Most participants quickly wiped out Tanaland's population, but a few were able to preserve a healthy rate of growth. The differences between the experiment's two groups, Dörner wrote, were striking: "The good participants acted *more complexly.* Their decisions took different aspects of the entire system into account, not just one aspect. This is clearly the more appropriate behavior in dealing with complicated systems," he added, because complexity means there are "many interdependent variables in a given system," which makes "it impossible to undertake only one action."

Dörner continued, "To the ignorant, the world looks simple. If we pretty much dispense with gathering information, it is easy for us to form a clear picture of reality and to come to clear decisions based on that picture." Further, "The bad participants displayed...a reluctance to gather information and an eagerness to act. By contrast, the good participants were initially cautious about acting and tried to secure a solid base of information.... The less information gathered, the greater the readiness to act."

Moving your focus

Complex action requires an ever-moving focus, which involves:

- Solving the problem that needs to be solved, which means resisting the temptation to do only what you enjoy doing or only what you are good at doing.
- To the degree you can, tackling problems while they are still small. I'm thinking of the children's book *The Little Prince,* in which the prince is looking for a sheep to help him with his baobab-tree problem. When told that the trees are enormous, he points out that they start small.
- Shifting your focus from the big picture to the details and back again without fixating at just one level of the problem.
- Balancing the need to gather more information with the need to get something done.

To return to the example of your becoming a doctor, suppose you are an emergency room physician. One day your tea-stained friend, who has been in a car wreck, is wheeled in. First you'd make sure his airway is clear and that his breathing and circulation are fine (details and action), but all the while you would keep an eye on his vital signs (big picture and information). At the same time that all of this is going on, you would attend to his emotional needs and try to moderate your emotional reaction at seeing your friend in such a state. Definitely very difficult to do, but you have to do it all at once to achieve the best outcome.

Gathering feedback

Gathering feedback is important because it allows you to test your understanding of the problem you are trying to solve. Even more important, it helps you to make sure you are solving the right problem. Drucker says that quality isn't what you put into a thing: it is what somebody else gets out of it. He is right, right in the irritating way that natural selection is right. If nature allows the saber-toothed tiger to go extinct while the roach flourishes, which is more fit? If nobody buys an obviously better product, then is it truly better? If you tell a joke and nobody laughs, then is it funny? The question to consider is: Who defines the outcome? I don't get to say whether I am a good husband, a good father, a good teacher, a good consultant; only feedback from my wife, son, students, and clients counts as an answer.

It is, of course, not enough simply to *collect* feedback. You must allow the most recent information to inform—that is, to change—your actions. You must allow for the possibility that the next thing you learn can change everything. Suppose that you went to medical school so you could become a doctor, because you wanted to help people. Unfortunately, while in medical school you discovered that you have an atrocious diagnostic sense, but a real gift for virology. You'd be a fool to ignore this feedback. You could continue to pursue the goal of helping people, but change it to help people by fighting the viruses that ail them.

Employing redundancy

Efficiency entails using the minimum resources to maximum effect; redundancy involves over-determining the outcome. The problem with efficiency is that if any link in the efficient chain breaks, the chain fails and the goal falls to its doom. Redundancy is the opposite of efficiency. It entails intentionally using more than the minimum resources necessary to achieve an effect, which helps to guarantee that you will achieve the desired outcome.

A break in a link may cost you one chain, but if you have multiple chains, it doesn't matter. In fact you shouldn't have just chains, but ropes, cables, and straps, because the type of problem that can break one chain could break all chains. It is, however, less likely to break things of different natures. Call this *heterogeneous redundancy*, which is to generate different kinds of causes that will all lead to the same results. If you're a general, you should be able to supply your troops by land, sea, and air so that if the land route is cut, you can still feed them, which, as the Prussian general von Clausewitz recommended in *On War*, should happen "almost every day."

Engaging in *K*-selection

Think of a mosquito. It uses an evolutionary reproductive strategy called *r*-selection. With *r*-selection an animal creates as many offspring as it can, invests little in each, and plays the odds. Some, at least, are going to make it. The opposite of *r*-selection is *K*-selection, in which an animal has few offspring and invests a lot in each. Picture an orangutan.

Legendary stock investor and billionaire Warren Buffett follows a *K*-selection strategy. Buffett has said that investing well isn't a matter of how big your circle of competence is, but of how clear you are on the boundary of that circle. Buy a stock when you are sure it will increase in value. Otherwise, be patient. It's not about smarts, but discipline. You could become rich if you were allowed to make only twenty stock purchases in your entire life, according to Buffett, because such a constraint would force you to choose carefully, an approach that Buffett has labeled *strategic inaction.*

Ted Williams, the last baseball player to bat over .400, was also a *K*-strategist. He calculated that there were seventy-two different paths along which a ball could pass through his strike zone. He reckoned that he could hit five of them—and he swung at *only* those five. Deciding what *not* to do is crucial. Drucker recommended that you should not only set your priorities, you should also set your posteriorities, or that which you will *not* do. Management consultant Tom Peters has called this having not just a to-do list, but also a to-don't list.

The strategy of *K*-selection is akin to that of the Prussian king Frederick the Great's observation that "Those generals who have but little experience attempt to protect every point, while those who are better acquainted with their profession, having only the capital object in view, guard against a decisive blow, and acquiesce in smaller misfortunes to avoid greater." You allow many opportunities to slip past, but you seize the few that matter. The trick is to err well within your circle of competence. This forces clarity of purpose on your actions and helps to guarantee that you do not waste resources.

Acquiring foreknowledge

One way to increase your efficacy is to know the outcome before you attempt a task. But how do you obtain such foreknowledge? One way is to choose which side you will err on. Suppose it usually takes you half an hour to get to work, but one day you have an important meeting scheduled early in the day. So you leave for work an hour and a half early. By guaranteeing that you arrive too early, you have foreknowledge that you'll be at the meeting on time.

Another avenue to foreknowledge is to choose *before* a situation arises how you will handle it. You can see this with a thought experiment: no matter what happens at work today, make certain you leave by five o'clock. By committing to do this, you have accurately predicted the future. The more general point is that as you increase your ability to choose your reactions to various situations or stimuli, you gain knowledge of the future. By deciding beforehand what is on both your to-do list and your to-don't list, you know something about the future—namely that you won't be swinging at the sixty-seven pitches that even Ted Williams couldn't hit.

Foreknowledge is an effective tactic because it changes the nature of the task. It decreases the demands on you in the particular moment. Having already decided what to do, you no longer have to think about it and thus can put your attention elsewhere, such as on executing the task, rather than dividing your attention between deciding and executing. The key to martial arts sparring is to realize that when you attack, your opponent will freeze, attack, or retreat. If he freezes, you punch. If he attacks, you block and jab. If he retreats, you lunge and jab. Then practice each of these moves a thousand times, so that when you face an opponent, you don't have to think about what to do. Then do the same with kicks, elbow strikes, and all other attacks. Eventually, you will map the entire space of everything that could happen, and you will have practiced every inch of it—that is, you will have developed foreknowledge—so that no matter what your opponent does, you can respond at the speed of thought.

The power of foreknowledge is why it is the central focus of *The Art of War* and why Sun Tzu emphasized that "The victorious first win and then engage the battle. Losers engage the battle and then seek to win."

Calculating comparative advantage

Opportunity cost is the next best alternative you could have had with your time or money. It is that which you give up by choosing what you chose. The opportunity cost of going to school is the money you could have made while you were in school (a sum usually surpassed within a few years of completing school). *Absolute advantage* comes from being better at doing something than someone else. If you were a virologist, then you might be faster at setting up lab equipment than your research assistant. *Comparative advantage* combines opportunity cost and absolute advantage. Even though you are faster at setting up lab equipment, you should still have your research assistant set it up, because if you set it up, then you are not spending the same time performing the analysis, which only you can perform and which adds more value.

Trading problems

Bridge the gap between your circle of competence and the demands of the world by trading problems with people who have the skills to solve the problems you can't. It would be easy to underestimate how useful this approach is, but Robert Kelly's research in *How to Be a Star at Work* found it to be the single most decisive factor in separating the best from the rest. You help others with their problems and they help you with yours. Suppose you did become a virologist. Using this tactic, you would go out of your way to help colleagues with their work, such as researching the virological causes of cancer. Then, when you became stuck on a problem—for example, trying to assess if viruses progress differently in children than in adults—you could ask for help from the people you'd helped. Because you'd helped them, they'd be more likely to help you.

Applying what you know

Make your circle of competence speak to the problem. This is akin to how people use myths. Historian of religions Jonathan Z. Smith drew on anthropologist Victor Turner's work in divination to explain how myths are similar to wine. People can make wine from nearly any fruit but typically make wine only from grapes. Yet from that initial reduction in choices (from any fruit to just grapes), there then follows a great expansion in that there are thousands of different kinds of wines, all made from grapes. From "an almost limitless horizon of possibilities that are at hand," said Smith, the field of possible cultural meanings is reduced to the fixed set of meanings that are contained in the myth. In other words, myths are often a small number of stories that people tell again and again.

"Then," Smith elaborated, "the most intense ingenuity is exercised to overcome the reduction" when people apply these cultural meanings to deal with a problem. That is, even though there are a small number of stories in the myth, people make these stories speak to an ever-increasing number of different circumstances. People apply ancient sutras to decisions on biotechnology; they ask the Bible to speak to issues of nuclear proliferation. In other words, your circle of competence may be quite small, but by exercising it creatively, you can apply it to many problems.

Summary

The efficient cause is concerned with taking action to get results, particularly in a complex and dynamic world such as ours. Think again of Nurse Bryan. Patients on her floor did better and recovered faster than patients on other floors; that is, she got results. Nurse Bryan mastered the efficient cause of patient care. Effective action in a complex world requires considered action—knowing when and how to take action and when not to. But on what do you base your actions? The material cause addresses the issue of your most important resources.

III

Your Resources
MATERIAL CAUSE

The exercise of the virtues is itself a crucial component of the good life.

—ALASDAIR MACINTYRE

Material cause involves what you have to work with—your resources. Perhaps you command legions or can throw millions of dollars at a problem. Perhaps not. Whatever other resources you may have (or may lack), you unquestionably have a mind. Indeed, if you have read this far, then you have the capacity to acquire enough material cause to make a lasting contribution, so I'll focus on you and what you can do with your mind. In their book, *Why We Want You to be Rich*, Donald Trump and Robert Kiyosaki hold a similar view of mind-as-resource. They noted, "Putting...ideas into action will require resources. So we're back to your...intelligence, also known as your...skills."

In the previous chapter I wrote that to make a lasting contribution is difficult, because the world is an open dynamic system. You can overcome this difficulty because your mind is also an open dynamic system. You can interact with the world and become more sophisticated in your thoughts and actions. In this sense, your most valuable resource is captured with the Greek word *aretê* [ar-uh-tay] (αρετή), from Greek, meaning *virtue* or *excellence*. The more *aretê* you have to work with, the more you can achieve. There are three aspects of *aretê* that are particularly helpful in striving to make a lasting contribution—perception, expertise, and mastery.

Perception

People do not perceive primarily with their senses, but with their minds. Psychologist Egon Brunswik and others have shown that people often don't see a thing unless they have some idea of what they are looking for. The reason for this may be biological. In *On Intelligence*, Jeff Hawkins and Sandra Blakeslee wrote that "for every fiber feeding information forward into the neocortex, there are ten fibers feeding information back toward the senses." Where most people see an undifferentiated mass of green leaves, a bird watcher spots a toucan, three species of parrots, and a hummingbird. Since I've been trained in statistics, I see the familiar bell-shaped curve when I look at skid marks on runways, smudges on doors, and wear patterns in carpets.

The need to cultivate your perception is even more important when it comes to seeing abstract ideas. I think this may have been what the *New York Sun* had in mind in 1897 when the paper's editors responded to young Virginia's question as to whether there really is a Santa Claus:

> The most real things in the world are those that neither children nor men can see.... Nobody can con-

ceive or imagine all the wonders there are unseen and unseeable in the world.

You tear apart the baby's rattle and see what makes the noise inside, but there is a veil covering the unseen world which not the strongest men, nor even the united strength of all the strongest men that ever lived could tear apart. Only faith, poetry, love, romance can push aside that curtain and view and picture the supernal beauty and glory beyond. Is it all real?.... [I]n all this world there is nothing else real and abiding.

This makes me wonder what I don't see because I lack the words, such as the following example of a concept from Christopher Moore's book *In Other Words*:

From Hungarian: *egyszer volt budán ktyavásár* [egdzair volt bood-an koocha-vah-sha] (idiom) An enigmatic Hungarian idiom that literally translates as 'there was a dog-market in Buda only once.' The meaning in English is close to 'a favorable opportunity that only happens once.' It is something to be grasped with two hands, otherwise you will find yourself regretting it at a later date.

Nor must you leave English to find concepts that, once learned, help you to see through the glass less darkly. Anthropologist Alexander Goldenweiser gives an example with the word *involution*. Involution happens when a system has developed to a point when it should move to the next stage, but fails to and so grows inward, becoming ever more complex. Late Gothic art, with its ornateness, is one example. Or, compare Bach's complexity with Beethoven's expansiveness. I think of involution when I see the wild tricks city kids do on skateboards and bicycles—Misty Flips, nose pokes, tail whips, and X-Ups. Would they perform such tricks if they had broad open spaces in which to skate and ride?

You can cultivate your ability to perceive through practice. Ray Bradbury contended:

> I believe that eventually quantity will make for quality.
>
> How so?
>
> Michelangelo's, da Vinci's, Tintoretto's billion sketches, the quantitative, prepared them for the qualitative, single sketches further down the line, single portraits, single landscapes of incredible control and beauty.
>
> A great surgeon dissects and re-dissects a thousand, ten thousand bodies, tissues, organs, preparing thus by quantity the time when quality will count—with a living creature under his knife.
>
> An athlete may run ten thousand miles in order to prepare for one hundred yards.
>
> Quantity gives experience. From experience alone can quality come.

Because conception leads perception, you have to cultivate your inner eye. In this sense, beauty is not the only intangible that is in the eye of the beholder. You must look with your eyes, but see with your mind. Listen with your ears, but hear with your heart. When you do, you will see into the world more deeply:

- Before you've ever thrown a punch, an expert martial artist can tell by your stance whether you have been trained.
- An owl's nest, if read properly, speaks to the health of a forest.
- That cloud means rain.
- Comparing their sales to their profits, I'd say that their stock is about to crash.

Your powers of perception will allow you to see and seize opportunities that others miss. Hotel magnate Kemmons Wilson capitalized on the knowledge that "Opportunity comes often. It knocks as often as you have an ear trained to hear it, an eye trained to see it, a hand trained to grasp it, and a head trained to use it."

Expertise

When scientists began to study expertise, they first assumed that experts must be smarter or more talented than novices, but they quickly learned that the key difference between experts and novices is not mental power, but knowledge. Cognitive psychologists Michelene Chi, Marshall Farr, and Robert Glaser have defined an expert as somebody who has a great deal of highly organized domain-specific knowledge, where a domain is a network of knowledge, such as chess, mathematics, or music. For experts, knowledge has morphed from many pieces into a unified whole. An expert can start with any piece of knowledge and explain how it fits with every other piece. I always picture the way Sherlock Holmes could start with a soil stain and, through a chain of reasoning, solve the case.

Understanding other people's expertise can help you

develop your own. Surprisingly, experts make mistakes, but experts catch and correct their mistakes faster than do novices. Experts take a long time to make sure they understand a problem. If you give an expert and a novice the same problem, the novice will immediately begin to try to solve it. The expert will reflect on the nature of the problem. From the outside, it will appear as if the expert is doing nothing and the novice is making progress. Once the expert understands the problem, she can solve it better and faster than can the novice.

Understanding expertise also helps you see where intuition comes in: it comes last. Experts do use intuition to solve problems, but it is a cultivated intuition resulting from at least 20,000 hours of on-task study. Intuition works as a guide only after experts have saturated themselves with their field's knowledge. Herbert Simon described expertise as follows:

> Counts have been made of the number of "friends" that chess masters have: the numbers of different configurations of pieces on a chessboard that are old familiar acquaintances to them. The estimates come out, as an order of magnitude, around fifty thousand, roughly comparable to vocabulary estimates for native speakers. Intuition is the ability to recognize a friend and to retrieve from memory all the things you've learned about the friend in the years you've known him. And of course if you know a lot about the friend, you'll be able to make good judgments about him. Should you lend him money or not? Will you get it back if you do? If you know the friend well, you can say "yes" or "no" intuitively.

Nobel laureate Luis "Luie" Alvarez provides an example of how to learn the language of a domain. Alvarez and his son, Walter, were the first scientists to suggest that an asteroid killed the dinosaurs. The clue was a dusting of iridium, an isotope that is rare on earth but common in asteroids. As soon as Alvarez saw it, he knew it was significant; but *how* did he know? Alvarez's biographer Richard Rhodes wrote that for years, Alvarez ran the only cyclotron in the world: "On a wall in the laboratory the young physicists put up a big board laid out with the periodic table, with hooks projecting from the boxes designating elements, and each time someone identified a new isotope, Luie labeled a wooden tag with the isotope's characteristics and hung the tag from the appropriate hook. That's how he got to know isotopes so well. The knowledge he derived from those hard early years of work stayed with him like a vocabulary for the rest of his life." In short, you are an expert in your field when you know its vocabulary and grammar as well as you know that of your native language.

Mastery

I think of mastery in the way Japanese think of *sasuga* [sa-sü-ga] (流石), the idea that if you are a master of one thing, then you are a master of all things. This idea has ancient roots, beginning in China in the sixth century with the *Chan** practice of seeking enlightenment by pondering *koans* [ko-an] (公案). A *koan* is the Japanese word for the Chinese *gong-an* [gäng-an], or *case*, as in *a legal case* or *precedent*. Buddhist scholar D. T. Suzuki's

Tad Waddington

---

*The word *Chan* (禅) comes from the Sanskrit *dhyana*, but is better known in the West by the Japanese word *Zen*.

famous example of a *koan* is, "What is the sound of one hand clapping?" To understand it, Suzuki wrote, you should "Devote yourself to it day and night, whether sitting or lying, whether walking or standing; devote yourselves to its solution during the entire course of the [day]. Even when dressing or taking meals, or attending to your natural wants, you have your every thought fixed on the *koan*. Make resolute efforts to keep it always before your mind."

The value of such an intense focus is that it allows you to master something, even if what you master is infinitesimal. The understanding of mastery can then act as a guide to tackling new tasks. For example, any child can finger paint. To paint well, however, you must learn the rules of the craft, and eventually get those rules down to a science. Japanese students of painting did not begin by trying to paint something as complex as a bamboo shoot. Instead, they began by mastering a very small technique, such as painting a straight line. Zen scholars Omori Sogen and Terayama Katsujo wrote, "The basis of Oriental calligraphy and painting is the line. Traditionally, students of both disciplines were instructed to spend a minimum of three years concentrating on the brushing of straight lines."

Of course, just learning the rules won't make you a true master. Painting by numbers can only take you so far. To paint a beautiful line, you have to know how to break the rules; you have to learn how to get the rules down to an art. Still, even the artful breaking of a few rules, however, does not a true master make. You can only paint an exquisite line when you achieve *muga* [mü-ga] (含偶). *Muga*, concluded American anthropologist Ruth Benedict, is "a state of expertness in which there is no break, *not even the thickness of a hair* between a man's will and his act." You have mastered painting a line when you have left the rules behind. Or, to stretch the idiom, from first getting the rules down to a science, and then getting them down to an art, you must ultimately get them down to a religion—that is, Zen. Since Zen is the offspring of Daoism and Buddhism, it is perhaps not surprising that the ancient Daoist essayist Zhuangzi once wrote, "What I care about is the Dao, which goes beyond skill."

Once you have reached mastery in the small matter of the straight line, you are ready to practice painting a curved line. But this time you have an advantage. It is easier. Having achieved mastery once, you have a sense of how it feels, and this sense can guide you as you tackle new tasks. When learning to paint a curved line, you know what to look for; you know that you seek *muga* and that you can accomplish it. You have gained a taste of excellence, a sense of mastery, a nose for *aretê*. As the eighteenth-century Chinese art essayist Shen Tsung-ch'ien affirmed, "Once this is mastered, the skill so acquired can be freely applied to other objects."

Tad Waddington

Summary

The material cause involves the resources that you can use to bring about a lasting contribution. Think of Nurse Bryan. To have had the effect she had, she must have been a master of her craft, of the material cause. In many ways, the material cause is less concerned with your material assets than with how you cultivate yourself. I know millionaires who contribute little, particularly given that they have far more resources than did, say, Nelson Mandela during the 27 years he was locked up in South Africa's prisons. Consequently, it is important to cultivate yourself so you can seize the opportunities offered by the Buda dog-market. Next, you need a way to make full use of your *aretê*. The formal cause is that way.

IV

The Design of Action
FORMAL CAUSE

It's not wise to violate the rules until you know how to observe them.

—T. S. ELIOT

The formal cause has to do with the essence of what you seek to cause. Consider it the in-*form*-ation of your action, the *form*-ula for success. In Greek, it is the *logos* (λόγος). Logos supplies the *-ology* in epistemology, mythology, and teleology. It is the root word of *logic*. It means *word, reason, plan,* but also the *point,* as in "what's the point?" It's the big picture. In the Bible, the original Greek for John 1:1, "In the beginning was the Word," is, "In the beginning was the logos." So in the beginning was the formal cause. The Chinese translation of the Bible reads, "In the beginning was the Dao (道)." Similarly, in Japanese, *Do* [dō] (道) is what it means to be a thing, for example, *bushido* (武士道) is what it means to be a warrior.

Plans

More concretely, the formal cause is your plan for putting your resources into play in the service of your goal. The formal cause is an important part of your effort to make a lasting contribution, because it changes the nature of the equation. Think of the checklist a pilot uses before she takes off. If she is certain that she will never be distracted and will never make a mistake, then she doesn't need a checklist. Knowing, however, that few people are perfect all of the time, she sensibly decides to use a list that was prepared by experts. Now she simply has to do what is on the checklist, which is easier than remembering what to do and then doing it. A good plan helps you to make a lasting contribution, because it gives you a view of the big picture, which helps you with goal coherence, resource allocation, and risk assessment.

Goal coherence

Planning should help you map your goals so they include not only what you are trying to accomplish, but also the bad things you want to prevent from happening, as well as the existing good things that you want to keep from disappearing. To do this, you must consider the bigger picture. The U.S. invasion of Afghanistan provides an example. The colors red and yellow both stand out in daylight, but yellow is more visible than red in dim light, such as at dusk and dawn. To make sure Afghani civilians didn't accidentally step on unexploded cluster bombs, the military wrapped them in yellow plastic. Unfortunately, following this same logic, in an effort to make air-dropped food packages easier to find, these were also wrapped in yellow plastic. Only after scores of people, many of them children, died did the U.S. military realize that it should package the bombs and food in different colors. Bigger-picture planning would have prevented this tragedy.

Birds offer another example. Most birds time the hatching of their eggs for when food is most abundant. Since most birds follow this strategy, competition for food is also most fierce at that time. A few bird species hatch early, when there is less food but also much less competition for the available food. By factoring in more than one variable, these birds end up with more food for their young.

Resource allocation

A plan helps to show you what is possible and what is not. Of all the things you *can* do, the plan will tell you what you *must* do to succeed, as well as what you can, if necessary, do without. It will tell you what you must do first and what you can safely put off until later. It makes you aware of milestones that help you track progress and provide feedback on how you are doing.

Your plan can also help you to save resources, because it can show you unexpected geodesics. A *geodesic* is the shortest distance between two points, but it isn't necessarily a straight line. The shortest distance may be counterintuitive. Think of a London taxi driver. Her destination may be one block away, but given the layout of the city, including one-way streets, the shortest path may involve five turns and, for a while, moving *away* from her destination. When you take the big picture into consideration and look at how all the pieces fit together, the shortest distance between you and your goal may be an unexpected path.

Risk assessment

Because it is in the nature of things to go wrong, you should use your plan to help you think ahead to figure out how you will deal with problems. Good planners engage in extensive what-if analyses (what some call "Project Tetris"), in which they figure out every possible combination of what to do should any given problem occur. The trick is to plan for things you think will *not* happen. That way you won't be surprised when the unexpected happens. "Who needs lifeboats," reasoned the designers of the *Titanic,* "on a ship that can't sink?"

Part of a good plan involves building in ways to get information about when your way of doing things is not working. For example, the explosion of the space shuttle *Challenger* in 1986 should have told NASA that the agency needed to stop overriding engineers' safety concerns in favor of staying on schedule. Because NASA did not change its fundamental way of doing business, the space agency stayed fixated on maintaining a schedule of launches and ignored engineers' warnings about possible damage to *Columbia's* heat shields. In 2003, right on schedule and in line with engineers' concerns, *Columbia* disintegrated on re-entry due to heat shield failure.

A good plan helps to keep you from becoming a captive of the moment, hence Nobel laureate Bertrand Russell's observation, "I think the essence of wisdom is emancipation, as far as possible, from the tyranny of the here and the now."

Documentation

To help you make your plan more useful, write it down. A good written plan should contain at least the following five elements:

1. The *final cause*: What your goal is—either the problem you seek to solve or the *aretê* you seek to manifest in the world.
2. The *material cause*: What resources you need to achieve your goal.
3. The *efficient cause*: What action you must take to achieve your goal.
4. *Risk assessment*: What could go wrong and what you can do about it.
5. *Feedback*: What feedback you require to learn whether you are getting the desired results.

Done properly, this document will allow you to know your options at all times. Think of the *muga* of the martial-arts master who has mapped the entire outcome-space of everything that might happen in a fight.

Beyond planning, the formal cause also entails the essence and information of the lasting contribution you seek to cause.

Essences

Since essences are constituted by details and there is no such thing as an essence of an essence, I'll use seven examples to show that focusing on the structure of something can help you understand it.

People

Reporter and historian Theodore H. White explained his thinking about the essence of people:

> You could separate people out into the large and the small...by whether their identities came from their own ideas or from the ideas of others. Most ordinary people lived their lives in boxes, as bees did in cells. It did not matter how the boxes were labeled: President, Vice President, Executive Vice President, Chairman of the Board, Chief Executive Officer, shop steward, union member, school teacher, policeman, "butcher, baker, beggar man, thief, doctor, lawyer, Indian chief," the box shaped their identity. But the box was an idea. Sir Robert Peel had put London policemen on patrol one hundred fifty years ago and the "bobbies" in London or the "cops" in New York now lived in the box invented by Sir Robert Peel. The Sterling Professor at Yale and the great physicists at the Cavendish Laboratory in Cambridge, England, alike lived in a box, labeled by someone else's idea. When a pilot awoke in the morning, he could go to the air strip feeling that he was the hottest pilot in the whole air force—but he was only a creation of Billy Mitchell's idea. And even if he was the bravest astronaut in outer space, he was still a descendant in identity from Robert Hutchings Goddard's idea of rocketry....

Whenever White met somebody, he said he'd ask himself, "Whose idea was he?" Perhaps this is why in *The Ascent of Man,* mathematician Jacob Bronowski mused,

Lasting Contribution

"We feel as if the ideas discover man, rather than the other way around."

Emergent properties

Some things change their nature when they interact with other things. Think of water, which is a liquid but is composed of two gases. Elements at one level of a system create properties at another level that differ from the elements that created them. Blind self-interest creates the invisible hand of the marketplace, which can work for the greater good. Neurons (which are not conscious) produce conscious minds. Simple rules produce complex behavior, as with an ant colony. Ones and zeros in your computer produce pixels on your monitor, which can be assembled to represent images, which can constitute the Mona Lisa's smile on your screensaver.

Understanding

In *Truth and Method,* philosopher Hans Georg Gadamer explained how people come to understand texts. This is an ancient problem, for philosophers have long known that you can't fully understand the individual sentences of a text until you understand the whole text—the context in which they occur. At the same time, however, you can't understand the whole text unless you understand the individual sentences. Gadamer solved the problem—called the *hermeneutic circle*—by realizing that the meaning of a text does not come from the text. Nor does it come from the reader. Nor does the text's meaning come from trying to figure out the author's intentions. Like an emergent property, meaning arises from an interplay, or dialectic, between the reader and the text. Because both you and the text exist in time and space, you start reading the text with some dim understanding. The words shape your understanding and your understanding shapes how you interpret the words. The interplay of your initial understanding and the text leads to deeper understanding. You do not find the text's "true meaning," because it does not exist. Instead, you achieve understanding, which is the ability to apply the text to new situations.

Take, for example, the children's book *The Little Engine That Could*, the story of a small switch engine that is called on to pull a big freight train over a mountain. The engine doubts its ability to carry out the task, but bucks itself up for the effort by saying, "I think I can, I think I can." The meaning of this text for a child may involve her using "I think I can" to help her overcome self-doubt and take on increasingly challenging tasks.

Two things follow from this observation. First, it shows that your actions can have effects that last. Actions have an ever-expanding cone of meaning and, therefore, can create results that echo through time. When a town in Massachusetts named itself Franklin, to honor Benjamin Franklin, Ben thanked them by giving them a library. This library was the foundation of Horace Mann's education. Mann became the first great advocate of public education in the United States, and widespread public education has been a primary driver of American prosperity for over a hundred years.

Second, meaning exists in application. If you learn something and never apply it, then in practice it is no different from never having learned it. Among other things, this means that the quality of the book you are reading exists outside the book. It exists in you, in what you do with it, and in how you use it as a formal cause toward your lasting contribution, because, as British historian Thomas Carlyle posited, "The best effect of any book is that it excites the reader to self-activity."

Yes and no

The structure of a problem may imply that the best approach is not to treat all potential answers equally. Obviously, a good salesperson doesn't take "no" for an answer. Not so obviously, a good thinker does not take "yes" for an answer. Obviously, if you fall off a roof, you approach the ground. Einstein was not hasty to accept this obvious answer and exercised the power of interpretation on this problem, which led him to the theory of relativity—because, not so obviously, you can also view the problem as the ground approaching you. In a sense—either from the point of view of physics or from the point of view of getting hurt—it doesn't matter whether you are approaching the ground or it is approaching you.

Minimax

Many decisions have characteristics that resemble games. The mathematician John von Neumann developed a general approach to games that can help you figure out a strategy in such situations. His method involves:

1. Looking at all the possible outcomes of a decision.
2. Determining the worst outcome.
3. Making certain the worst doesn't happen.

Because this strategy minimizes your maximum loss, it is called *minimax*. An important feature of this strategy is that it ignores the probability of different outcomes. The worst outcome may only have a 2 percent chance of happening, but with minimax you can be 100 percent certain that it won't happen.

For example, suppose your company gave you a bunch of stock; suppose that you have a mortgage. Minimax says that the worst outcome would be for the stock to become worthless. If this happened, you would lose the money in the stock and still have a mortgage. The minimax strategy says you should sell the stock and apply it to your mortgage. You probably will not maximize your gain, because the stock price may yet go up, but you've locked in some benefit and definitely prevented losing the value of the stock they gave you and further decreased the chance of losing your house. Quite a number of former Enron employees wish they had adopted this strategy.

Backward and forward

Some events are structured in such a way that the only way forward is backward. Imagine that you are on a mountain peak and you see a higher peak in the distance that you want to climb. You must first climb down to go up, just as a bow must be drawn backward to shoot an arrow forward. People sometimes get stuck in what is called a local maxima (the first mountain), because they are unable to see the mountain in the distance (global maxima) or because they are unwilling to give up the heights they have already reached.

PhD

As you make progress toward a goal, it is not necessarily true that the next step will be similar to the previous steps. The last step of the formal cause can be unexpected. In the book *In Pursuit of the PhD*, William Bowen and Neil Rudenstine calculated that fewer than 65 percent of people who start PhD programs finish them. I think this result is partly because students don't understand the formal cause of earning a PhD. The last step of the process is *to contribute to knowledge,* which is unlike the previous steps. Elementary school is like learning to ride a tricycle. High school is like learning to ride a bicycle. College is like learning to drive a car. A master's degree is like learning to drive a racecar. Students often think that the next step is more of the same, like learning to fly an airplane. On the contrary, the PhD is like learning to *design* a new car. Instead of taking in more knowledge, you have to *create* knowledge. You have to discover (and then share with others) something that nobody has ever known before.

Information

If the formal cause involves the in-*form*-ation of an action, then what is information? Mathematician Claude Shannon's answer to this question gave humanity the mathematical underpinnings of the information age. The answer is surprising, because people often think of information as content that a sender puts into (encodes) a channel—like a tube—which the receiver then takes out (decodes) at the other end. This view is wrong, because information is not found in the sender, the channel, or the receiver. It isn't found anywhere, because information isn't a thing; it is a relation.

Let's say that I am uninformed, that I do not know whether Annie Oakley was a good shot. Where is the information that will inform me? It isn't in the bullets she shoots. Nor is it in the moving targets at which she shoots. Nor is it in her gun that tracks (or leads) the targets. Information exists in the relationship between the moving gun, the moving bullet, and the moving target; information exists in whether she hits the targets. Similarly, information isn't in the chocolate that I enjoy with my coffee; nor is it in my waistline. Information exists in the *relationship* between my chocolate intake and my varying waistline.

What sort of relationship is information? It is a reduction in the variability of a system, a decrease in chaos. Why, I might ask, is my waistline expanding? Is it bad karma? Lousy genes? Too much coffee? My random guessing continues until I consider how my waistline seems to change with the varying amounts of chocolate that I eat. Then my befuddlement, my random guessing, my system variation is reduced. Suppose I am confused about when Columbus sailed across the Atlantic. I guess wildly: 1422, 1490, 1500.... My variable responses continue until I look it up and read, "1492." The encyclopedia did not *contain* information about when Columbus sailed, but it did *inform* my response to the question. The next time I wonder about Columbus' voyage, I'll invariably answer, "1492."

The evolutionary biologist Stephen Jay Gould articulated the idea of variation as essence in his essay, "The

Median Isn't the Message," which explained how to think about statistical averages:

> The point is a subtle one, but profound—for it embodies the distinctive way of thinking in my own field of evolutionary biology and natural history.
>
> We still carry the historical baggage of a Platonic heritage that seeks sharp essences and definite boundaries. (Thus we hope to find an unambiguous "beginning of life" or "definition of death," although nature often comes to us as irreducible continua.) This Platonic heritage, with its emphasis in clear distinctions and separated immutable entities, leads us to view statistical measures of central tendency wrongly, indeed opposite to the appropriate interpretation in our actual world of variation, shadings, and continua. In short, we view means and medians as the hard "realities," and the variation that permits their calculation as a set of transient and imperfect measurements of this hidden essence.... But all evolutionary biologists know that variation itself is nature's only irreducible essence. Variation is the hard reality, not a set of imperfect measures for a central tendency. Means and medians are the abstractions.

Information is the process by which you interact with a system such that the result is reduced randomness or uncertainty. A blueprint helps to reduce the entropy in the process of building a house. A route plan helps reduce the chaos of going on a trip—if, that is, you follow the plans.

Summary

The formal cause is the DNA of action. It is the recipe for success, the rules of the game. Nurse Bryan's daily actions were organized around the formal cause, "Are we really making the best contribution to the purpose of this hospital?" The formal cause is the blueprint that tells you how to construct the causal chain from your values to your results. It is the road map that informs how to get from here to there. But where is *there* and why go? The *why* of action is addressed by the final cause.

V

Embody Your Goal
FINAL CAUSE

Nothing great in the world has been accomplished without passion.
—GEORG WILHELM FRIEDRICH HEGEL

The goal you are trying to achieve is the *final cause.* There are two kinds: from the outside in and from the inside out. With the outside-in, you observe a problem in the world and seek to solve it. Noah Webster published his dictionary as a way to create a common language that would unify the people of the early United States. In business, the outside-in is the marketing-focused company; customers need something, and you try to provide it. The inside-out approach starts with some form of *aretê* and seeks to apply it to the world. A musician can't get a tune out of her head. An engineer creates a nifty device. A teacher loves being around kids. In business, the inside-out is the product-focused company; you are a great innovator and you try to get customers to buy your products.

Being aware of the final cause helps you to make a lasting contribution, because it focuses your attention in the right places. French anthropologist Claude Lévi-Strauss' summary of mythical thought highlights the point:

The kind of logic which is used by mythical thought is as rigorous as that of modern science, and that the difference lies not in the quality of the intellectual process, but in the nature of the things to which it applies.... [T]he same logical processes are put to use in myth as in science, and man has always been thinking equally well; the improvement lies, not in an alleged progress of man's conscience, but in the discovery of new things to which it may apply its unchangeable abilities.

In other words, the end to which you think and work is at least as important as *how* you think and work.

Whether from the inside out or from the outside in, the final cause is the *why* of the action. It is future-oriented. Senge stated, "In every instance where one finds a long-term view actually operating in human affairs, there is a long-term vision at work. The cathedral builders of the Middle Ages labored a lifetime with the fruits of their labors still a hundred years in the future."

There is an underlying spirit to your actions, and that spirit captures the essence of the final cause. The final cause of washing your baby isn't just a clean baby; it is another way to show that you love the child. Final causes provide the motive force to your actions. Final causes should stoke the fires of your soul and provoke your passions, in the same way that Achilles' rage provided the first spark of the *Iliad*. The final cause can be an animating force, because, according to the poet Muriel Rukeyser, "The universe is made of stories, not atoms." In other words, in the realm you care about—

the human realm—the nature of the world matters less than the stories you tell yourself about the nature of the world.

The final cause provides a valuable motive force. Much is said about ancient Greek civilization and how its philosophy gave the West a boost through the ages. While this may be true, there was, I think, also something else going on. The ancient Greeks had skin in the game: they personally, viscerally, gave a damn. Intangible events were not mere abstractions to them. Discord didn't just happen: it was the goddess Eris causing trouble. And watch out for her brat, Strife. You didn't become wise with age: wisdom was a gift from Metis. You did not merely have second thoughts: Athena grabbed you by the hair and forced you to reconsider. For the ancient Greeks, *it was personal.* As for me, I do not merely exercise: I battle Sloth. I do not weed dandelions: I lead a safari. I don't struggle with self-doubt: I fight a fire-breathing, lion-headed, serpent-tailed chimera. My vorpal blade sings, "I think I can, I think I can." I don't just wish to be creative: I want to bed a muse, and not just any muse—Polymatheia!*

To be clear, I am suggesting a conscious mythologizing of the causal process, an exaggerating of intentions. I do so to give you the avatar's advantage and to help you impart a certain heroic quality to your actions.

Avatar's advantage

The final cause can give you the avatar's advantage. An avatar, from the Sanskrit *avatāra,* is the incarnation of a

*Fat chance.

deity in human form. An incarnation, according to the *Oxford English Dictionary,* is the fact of being "made flesh." John 1:1 continued, "In the beginning was the Word.... And the Word became flesh and dwelt among us...." The final cause entails *embodying* the idea of the thing you seek to cause. You manifest its logos. You become its avatar. How?

Ideas enter the world as hatchlings. They cannot live without care and feeding. They feed on sacrifice and action. You give life to them through your efforts. This is how Santa Claus, in a sense, came to life. Referring to this process, Confucius reflected that "It is not the Dao that makes people great; it is people who make the Dao great." Socrates died for Law. Millions have bled for Freedom. Artists have toiled for Beauty. Thousands of scientists have labored for Truth; millions of teachers, for Education. "Martyrs create faith," held philosopher Miguel de Unamuno; "faith does not create martyrs."

And yet Confucius and Unamuno are only half right. To understand why they are only half right, to demystify what I mean by the avatar's advantage, and to show how your actions can take on a life of their own, I'll draw on the research of sociologists Peter Berger and Thomas Luckmann. They explained that people often engage in a three-step process: people externalize, objectify, and internalize.

1. Externalize: in an effort to improve crop yields, somebody puts forward the clever idea of not digging thousands of holes to plant seeds, but of cutting the earth as though with a knife.

2. Objectify: the idea is forged into a solid object, a plow.
3. Internalize: once the plow has been around a while, it can impose its logic on people such that they always think of planting fields with a plow and no other way even occurs to them.

This process works with things more abstract than plows. Once, the concept of socialism was just words on paper (externalization). Then it became a form of government that imposed its logic on millions (objectification), some of whom could not think outside the bounds set by it (internalization). The 2001 Tour de France provides another example. Lance Armstrong and his closest rival, Jan Ullrich, were riding shoulder-to-shoulder. In such a tightly contested race, I expected these ferocious competitors to take advantage of *every* opportunity to win. Then Ullrich crashed. Armstrong pulled over and waited for Ullrich to get back in the race. When asked about this, Armstrong said that he couldn't imagine taking advantage of the situation: the etiquette of the sport demanded that he wait. Later Ullrich, in the lead, reached back to shake Armstrong's hand. On the one hand, Sportsmanship inspired their actions. On the other hand, their actions gave added life to Sportsmanship itself.

In short, the avatar's advantage involves creating an effect that takes on a life of its own, an effect that embodies the spirit of the contribution you seek to make. We give ourselves to an idea and it returns the favor. This is how ideas take wing. The dangerous part is that this process can work for good or ill. It becomes a vicious circle if you are empowering the wrong idea, such as slavery. It becomes a benevolent circle if you are empowering the right idea, such as human rights.

How does this work? In a sense, it works because you say it does. It works through constitutive rules.

Constitutive rules

Constitutive rules describe a way in which lower-level entities count as higher-level entities simply because you say they do. The philosopher John Searle contended:

> [S]ome rules do not merely regulate, they also create the very possibility of certain activities. Thus the rules of chess do not regulate an antecedently existing activity. It is not the case that there were a lot of people pushing bits of wood around on boards, and in order to prevent them from bumping into each other all the time and creating traffic jams, we had to regulate the activity. Rather, the rules of chess create the very possibility of playing chess. The rules are *constitutive* of chess in the sense that playing chess is constituted in part by acting in accord with the rules.

Searle cited marriage as an example. Saying certain words under certain conditions counts as making a promise, which under certain conditions, counts as a contract, which under certain conditions counts as a marriage, which is an institutional fact. Moreover, explained Searle, "[I]nstitutions are not worn out by continued use, but each use of the institution is in a sense a renewal of that institution. Cars and shirts wear out as we use them but constant use renews and strengthens institutions such as marriage, property, and universities." Searle went on:

> At this point, I am just calling attention to a peculiar logical feature that distinguishes social concepts from such natural concepts as "mountain" or "molecule." Something can be a mountain even if no one believes it is a mountain; something can be a molecule even if no one thinks anything at all about it. But for social facts, the attitude that we take toward the phenomenon is partly constitutive of the phenomenon. If, for example, we give a big cocktail party, and invite everyone in Paris, and if things get out of hand, and it turns out that the casualty rate is greater than the Battle of Austerlitz—all the same, it is not a war; it is just one amazing cocktail party. Part of being a cocktail party is being thought to be a cocktail party; part of being a war is being thought to be a war.

How does this relate to how people like you and me can make a lasting contribution? Searle gives the answer: "One way to impose a function on an object is just to start using the object to perform that function." Cooking dinner for somebody is an act of courtship if you say it is (and it isn't if you say it isn't). You impose a function (meaning) on an object (dinner) and begin to use your actions as the institution of courtship. In short, your actions can count as contributing, in part, because you say they do.

Heroic quality

Nothing I have said about making a lasting contribution should suggest to you that doing so is easy. The difficulty of accomplishing the task is why having a final cause of mythical proportions is important: it helps you to keep on keeping on. A good final cause gives you the motivation you need to succeed. It is the key to the unseen world of supernal beauty and glory, to that which is the most real and abiding.

You can think of the myth-making aspect of the final cause in the way that screenwriting teacher Robert McKee talked about "the Principle of Antagonism" in his book *Story*: "A protagonist and his story can only be as intellectually fascinating and emotionally compelling as the forces of antagonism make them." Odysseus' greatness rose to the level of the challenges he faced. Frodo was made great by the depth of Sauron's evil. See yourself as a hero in a story and every obstacle, rather than bringing you down, can draw out greater qualities of your character. Such mythologizing gives the heroic quality that British art historian Kenneth Clark wrote about in his book *Civilisation*:

> "I suppose that this quality, which I may call heroic, is not part of most people's idea of civilisation. It involves a contempt for convenience and a sacrifice of all those pleasures that contribute to what we call civilised life. It is the enemy of happiness. And yet we recognise that to despise material obstacles, and even to defy the blind forces of fate, is man's supreme achievement;...in the end, civilisation depends on man extending his powers of mind and spirit to the utmost...."

In their book *Built to Last,* Jim Collins and Jerry Porras wrote about what I've called a final cause as a BHAG, a Big Hairy Audacious Goal. A BHAG, a final cause of mythic stature, gives you the moxie, the chutzpah, the pluck you need to get a difficult job done. It shifts your focus from playing not to lose to playing to win, and from only conserving resources to maximizing the quality of the contribution you can make. This shift is important but subtle, so I'll try to point to it with four examples:

1. The best defense is a strong offense.
2. Think in terms of cultivating your perception. You are more likely to see a Buda dog-market if you are looking for one.
3. I'd rather chase a muse than be chased by a fury.
4. When you are on the attack (seeking to win), a failure is nothing but one less victory, but when you are playing defense, a failure is defeat.

Another advantage of mythologizing your actions and of giving them a heroic quality can be seen in the work of the religion scholar Mircea Eliade. He observed that for people to have meaningful lives they must put their lives into a narrative, a story, a myth. For example, because I love my family, I want to make sure they have enough food to eat and a place to live, so I, alas, must work for a living, which means that I have to drive to work. This means that I have to keep my car maintained, which means that I have to call to make an appointment with the service department. The receptionist puts me on hold and I am stuck listening to music that is dull enough to lull a young otter to sleep. Even though attending to the insipid music is a fifth-order derivative from my prime motivation of taking care of my family, my putting up with it is motivated by my deepest values. Knowing this makes tolerating it, well, tolerable. Mythologizing your actions helps to sensitize you to what poet May Sarton has called "the sacramentalization of the ordinary."

Summary

The final cause embodies your values. It gives motive force, because it comes from what you value. The stronger the value, the greater the power of the final cause. The more clearly articulated the value, the better you can embody it through action. Returning to Nurse Bryan, that she was an avatar of Care-In-Action, an avatar whose spirit lived on long after the flesh was gone, is evident in how she set standards that survived beyond her retirement. As the end (in the sense of *goal*), the final cause is, paradoxically, the *beginning* of how to make a lasting contribution. It motivates the entire process and raises your mundane actions to a higher level. But how can you be sure that the four causes are a sensible way to think about making a lasting contribution? The next two chapters address this question.

VI

Empirical Problems

Concepts are to be understood in terms of their practical implications.

—CHARLES S. PEIRCE

I have proposed a different way to think about action that, in its application, should help you to become more meaningfully effective. But no proposition—theory or application—should go unchallenged. To help you know whether I have written anything of value, I'll take a step back to answer critical questions. But first, if no proposition should go unchallenged, then you should challenge the proposition that no proposition should go unchallenged. So why spend your time on this? Because part of the reason that people are ineffective is they base their actions on faulty knowledge; they do so because they either don't know that it is important to put what they think they know to the test or they do not know how to test it. The intent of this and the next chapter is to show you the degree of scrutiny to which you should subject all knowledge and to show you that after subjecting the four-cause theory of action to a high level of scrutiny, you can use it with greater confidence.

Another reason to spend time on questioning what I have proposed is that it is not enough to know that ——

a thing works: you should also understand how and why it works. A T-shirt sold by University of Chicago students states this clearly. The front reads, "That's all well and good in practice..." And the back reads, "...but how does it work in theory?" The rules of the road, for example, exist to keep people safe, but it is acceptable to break the rules under certain circumstances, such as when the only way to avoid getting flattened by an oncoming train is to run a red light. This is obvious, because drivers have a thorough understanding of the rules of the road and of their limits.

Finally, there is a poetic reason. It has to do with exerting the *will to know*. Think of Oedipus, who was destined to do horrible things but not to *know* that he had done them. What makes Oedipus a myth for the ages isn't the intertwining of violence and incest. The myth is great because the man exerted his will to learn the truth, even if learning that truth would be painful.

I have presented here a theory of causality for human action; but what good is a theory? According to General Clausewitz, just like a good plan, theory is a guide to action. It accompanies you on the journey and helps to point the way. It helps to organize action. Creative-thinking expert Edward de Bono offered an example: "A two-finger typist with hundreds of hours of practice is still a two-finger typist. A few hours learning touch typing would have made a huge difference. It is the same with thinking."

How should you evaluate this theory of action? Philosopher of science Larry Laudan explained that a theory should be evaluated by both the number of empirical problems it solves and how well it fits with existing theories. The theories of evolution and creationism can both explain the empirical problem of why men have nipples. But there is a glaring difference in how the two explanations fit with other theories. Evolution's explanation does not cause problems for the theory of evolution, because it fits seamlessly with other theories of biology and human development, which fit with theories of chemistry and physics, and so on. Human embryos start out as females; only after several weeks does the Y chromosome kick in. With creationism, however, you should wonder: since man is created in God's image, why does God need nipples?

If it is true that this four-cause theory is useful, then you should be able to use it to analyze a variety of human activities. It should help you to solve empirical problems, even one as simple as baking a cake. The material cause involves flour, sugar, and eggs. The formal cause relates to the recipe. The efficient cause concerns your actions in the kitchen to bake it. The final cause points to the reason for baking it, such as a birthday party. And the causes interact with each other. If you were planning to bake a chocolate cake, but are told— difficult to imagine though it may be—that the birthday girl doesn't like chocolate (a change in the final cause), then the material cause changes to exclude chocolate. You also use a different recipe (formal cause) and your actions in making the cake (the efficient cause) subsequently change.

The four causes can interact with each other in subtler ways. For example, I wrote earlier about complexity

Tad Waddington

as if it was entirely a nuisance, but it has its useful side as well. Complexity creates a buffered system, meaning that because it takes many causes to create an effect, a butterfly flapping its wings in Beijing will not bring about a blizzard in Buffalo. Airplanes don't crash because somebody makes a simple mistake. It usually takes several errors working together to bring a plane down.

This means that complexity creates background noise, which can act as useful information. For example, it is unlikely that the avalanche I imagined earlier would have led you to spill tea on your friend's new shirt, because you knew you were in the mountains where avalanches are possible and you would have been dimly aware of the rumbling of snow before you were consciously aware of it. You would have been forewarned and would not have been startled. Similarly, if you blow out a tire on your car, you won't necessarily be taken by surprise, because before it blows you will be vaguely aware of tire vibrations, and this awareness will help to prepare you for trouble.

The following examples show that you can use the theory to solve a variety of empirical problems.

Business

Given that Drucker defined management as a process of turning resources into results, the material cause is your resources. The formal cause is shown in the Venn diagram below. It consists of your competencies, your customers, and your competitors. Your business model is how you use your competencies to meet your customers' wants. Game theory is how you keep your competitors off balance. Strategy is how you meet your customers' wants while dealing with your competitors. Strategy is further constrained in that, as General Douglas MacArthur declared, the definition of victory is the first determinant of strategy. How you define victory is your final cause.

According to Jim Collins and Jerry Porras, the final cause is not to maximize shareholder value; the final cause is the company's mission. In *Built to Last*, they found that, in the long run, companies that had a purpose greater than profit outperformed those that were focused only on making money. They concluded: "Contrary to business school doctrine, 'maximizing shareholder wealth' or 'profit maximization' has not been the dominant driving force or primary objective through the history of the visionary companies. Yet, paradoxically, the visionary companies make more money than the more purely profit-driven comparison companies."

The efficient cause is how you execute your strategy. This is a challenge, because everything else in your business—your financial and organizational structures, for example—must adapt to your strategy. Since your competencies, your customers' wants, and your competitors' actions change over time, your strategy and therefore everything else you do must also change.

Common business clichés capture the four causes. "It's not the size of the dog in the fight; it's the size of the fight in the dog [final cause]." And, "You've got to play the hand you are dealt [material cause]." Finally, "Plan the work [formal cause] and work the plan [efficient cause]."

Oxford English Dictionary

The final cause is, "To be the last word on words." The material cause is some 2.4 million words. The efficient cause is thousands of people reading, researching, and writing. The formal cause, according to the 1933 edition, is, "To present in alphabetical series the words that have formed the English vocabulary from the time of the earliest records down to the present day, with all the relevant facts concerning their form, sense-history, and etymology."

Speeches

Your final cause is the change in the audience that you want to make. This means that you should be clear about what your goals are for giving the speech. And to help your audience understand what you are trying to communicate, you should make your message, to quote Einstein, "As simple as possible, but not simpler." You should also be clear about what is in it for them and shape your message in terms of their interests, their final causes.

Your material cause is not just the message you are trying to convey, but also the graphics, gestures, and eye contact that you use to convey your message. The material cause of a speech involves rhetoric and cognitive psychology. For example, people remember things that are presented first, last, and repeated, and that are meaningful, emotional, or unexpected.

Information theory constitutes the formal cause. It has to do with the relationship between your final cause and the change you bring about in the audience. That is, communication isn't what you say, but what the audience understands. This means that you should tell the audience how you have structured the information so they can more easily decode it.

Your giving of the speech is the efficient cause. You should state the key message in the opening and return to it in the closing. You should prepare two strong endings: one for the conclusion of the talk, and the other for the end of the question-and-answer session. To be safe, you should prepare a couple of questions with which to seed the question-and-answer session. Finally, you must be sensitive to the audience and adjust how you present your material to maximize the audience's ability to understand it.

Plot

Plot is the formal cause of a story. The Greek word for *plot* is *muthos,* from which we get our word *myth.* According to Aristotle, a well-plotted story must open with *energia* (energy, zip, bang). Recall Achilles' rage. The ending must be inevitable and a surprise. It is inevitable that Oedipus will fulfill the Oracle at Delphi's prophecy. The surprise is that he has already done so. The characters in the story are the material cause. The final cause is the moral of the story. The efficient cause is captured in the advice Richard Rhodes (whom you met earlier as Alvarez's biographer) received when he asked Hallmark Cards public relations manager Conrad Knickerbocker how to become a writer. Knickerbocker suggested, "Rhodes, you apply ass to chair." Rhodes remarked, "I call that solid advice *the Knickerbocker rule.*"

Career management

Ask yourself the following questions, most of which come from Drucker's *Harvard Business Review* article, "Managing Oneself." The final cause involves the answer to the questions: What do you seek to accomplish with your career? What are your goals, aspirations, desires, wishes, hopes? The material cause concerns the answers to: What are your strengths and weaknesses? How do you learn—by listening, doing, writing, talking? How do you perform—in a group or by yourself? The formal cause asks: What is your plan for achieving your goals? The efficient cause queries: What parts of your plan you will act on this year?

Wealth

According to Robert Kiyosaki's best-selling *Rich Dad* books on how to become wealthy, many people try to imitate the efficient cause of buying stocks or rental property. They fail because they haven't mastered the other three causes. They don't have the final cause of wanting financial freedom. Instead, they want security. Pursuing security, they are unwilling to take the risks necessary to achieve financial freedom. They don't understand that the material cause is the mind; money is an abstract concept that you see not with your eyes, but with your mind. Because people haven't trained their minds to understand how money works, they don't see opportunities—fleeting Buda dog-markets— when they arise. Finally, people don't understand that the formal cause of becoming rich is to acquire assets, where an asset is defined as anything that puts money in your pocket. For example, most people believe their banker when she says that their house is an asset. It *is* an asset—the banker's—because your mortgage puts money in the banker's pocket. If it isn't generating positive cash flow, then it isn't an asset. What, you may ask, about asset appreciation? Kiyosaki has three answers:

1. When you take inflation into consideration, assets usually aren't as good as they appear.
2. If the price of gold used to be $50 an ounce and is now $500, since the gold hasn't changed, has it increased in value or has your dollar become *less* valuable?
3. Well, OK, the typical definition of "asset" is anything that has value, but it is a powerful psychological trick you can play on yourself to define "asset" in terms of positive cash flow so that you don't blunder into bankruptcy by having too many "assets" and not enough cash.

Tad Waddington

The good life

Biologist T. H. Huxley held that, "The great end of life is not knowledge but action [efficient cause]." Bertrand Russell reflected, "The good life is one inspired by love [final cause] and guided [formal cause] by knowledge [material cause]."

Negative examples

The four-cause theory also explains the causes of failure. For example, research on small-business failures indicates that small-business owners work hard (efficient cause), want to succeed (final cause), and have business plans (formal cause), but run out of money and lack essential business skills (material cause). As a result, 90 percent fail in the first five years.

Alternatively, imagine you get lost while driving. You have a final cause: your destination. You have a material cause: the car. You have an efficient cause: your driving. It is your formal cause, your route, that is the problem.

Being all dressed up with no place to go is a failure of the final cause. Procrastination is a failure of the efficient cause, a failure to take action.

Generalizations

These examples yield a couple of insights. First, the formal cause is what you are asking for when you want to know the secret of how to do something. Take the example of a child and his architect grandfather playing with building blocks. The material cause (the blocks) is the same for both of them. The final cause (fun) is the same. The efficient cause (play) is the same. The critical difference is the formal cause. The child creates a hut and the grandfather the Taj Mahal, because the grandfather has a sophisticated blueprint for action.

Second, the gist of the four-cause theory is coordinated action. When you get all four causes to work together, you are more likely to succeed in your endeavors. Take a thought experiment as an example. Imagine that you have 12 points of effort to put into an action. Many people put all of their effort into the efficient cause and largely neglect the other three causes. This can be represented with the following:

Efficient cause = 9
Material cause = 1
Formal cause = 1
Final cause = 1

But since it is the output of the entire system that matters (which can be represented by the product of the elements), the result is 9 * 1 * 1 * 1 = 9 points of effect. On the other hand, if you were seeking to maximize the output of the system, you would allocate your effort differently:

Efficient cause = 3
Material cause = 3
Formal cause = 3
Final cause = 3

The result would be 3 * 3 * 3 * 3 = 81, a nine-fold increase in efficacy. This example suggests that you will get the greatest return for your efforts by not fixating on just one cause, but by harmonizing among all four.

Summary

One of the ways to measure the value of a theory is with the empirical problems it can solve. The examples above show that you can use the four-cause theory of human action to solve empirical problems. This is important, because what we care about, said physicist Georg Christoph Lichtenberg, is, "The fruits of the philosophy, not the philosophy itself." The next chapter explores how the theory of action fits with other theories.

VII

Theoretical Problems

The path of all knowledge leads through the question.

—HANS-GEORG GADAMER

But how does the theory fit with other theories? There are at least half a dozen tough questions you can ask of the theory and how to apply it to making a lasting contribution.

1. Science has spent the past several hundred years getting rid of the final cause. Plagues, for example, are no longer seen as divine punishment. The evolution of life wasn't toiling away all those years just to produce humans, so what is the final cause doing in this theory?
2. A four-cause theory lacks a certain elegance, and elegance in a theory matters; the general principle is Occam's Razor—that all else being equal, the simpler explanation is better. Isn't a four-cause theory three causes too many?
3. Is the theory true? In other words, how does it fit with how people define *truth*?
4. Is it realistic to say that an individual can make a lasting contribution?
5. Given that you might fail in your efforts to make a contribution that lasts, what role does failure play in the theory and in its application?

6. Don't you have to be a genius to make a lasting contribution?

Final cause revisited

The final cause is part of the theory for three reasons. First, you can't make sense of much of the world if you do not understand the role played by the final cause. Searle noted that "If you describe a car and leave out driving, you've left out something important." He went on to say, "Cars are for driving; dollars for earning, spending, and saving; bathtubs for taking a bath."

Second, because people have minds, the final cause is a necessary part of the causal process. From Searle's book *Intentionality*:

> Consider what it is like to learn how to ski. The beginning skier is given a set of verbal instructions as to what he is supposed to do: "lean forward," "bend the ankles," "keep weight on the downhill ski," etc. Each of these is an explicit representation, and, to the extent the skier is seriously trying to learn, each will function causally as part of the Intentional content determining the behavior. The skier tries to keep the weight on the downhill ski by way of obeying the instructions to keep weight on the downhill ski. Here we have a perfectly standard case of Intentional causation.

As you become a more adept skier, you can simply think, "go faster," and, in fact, speed up. Searle summarized the relationship between the material and final causes with, "Intentionality rises to the level of the background abilities." Think about somebody who has never driven a car. You must explain every little movement to her. As she learns, you explain less until you can just say, "It's your turn to drive." In other words, the more skill you have (material cause), the greater the scope your final cause can cover.

Third, the final cause provides motive power. How? Consider the case of a woman who bought a pair of Oprah Winfrey's shoes, even though the shoes didn't fit her. When she felt depressed and needed confidence, she stood in Oprah's shoes. She became confident enough to tell her story on national television, without the help of Oprah's shoes. Oprah as a role model was the final cause of her increased confidence. Given that there was no sole-to-soul magic that Oprah cast through her shoes to the woman, how did the final cause work?

Recall that information is a relation between sender and receiver. The shoes didn't vary, but her *interpretation of the meaning* of the shoes did. Because of the hermeneutic circle, you can't step into the same shoes twice; every time she revisited the shoes, she had experienced new things since the last time, and was bringing a new perspective and a new interpretation of her life to the shoes. Her varying interpretation of the shoes created the variation in the sender. The channel wasn't the shoes, but her thoughts. The variation in her confidence was the variation in the receiver. The relationship between sender and receiver created information, a decrease in system variability (her chaotic feelings), and an increase in her confidence. Although it seems that she got something from nothing, that she pulled herself up by her bootstraps, it was actually the hard work of her own thinking that accomplished the feat, as it were. This is why you should follow Unitarian minister William Ellery Channing's advice: "Be true to your own highest convictions." These convictions can help provide motive power to your actions.

This same process also explains how believers get a boost from faith. God is defined as *perfect.* As such, God cannot change or vary, because any change would imply less perfection either before or after the change; therefore God cannot be a source of information, and yet many people draw strength from their belief in God. This strength comes from the dynamic of the evolving interpretation of the relationship between the believer and God.

Inelegance

Elegance is one of the ways to judge a theory, but the four-cause theory of action appears to be inelegant. It's lumpy. On the one hand, it advocates overkill (through redundancy) in seeking to guarantee the desired outcome. On the other hand, it advocates small-domain specialization, a kind of underkill. How are these reconciled?

Overkill seems wasteful, but you can see throughout history that an overabundance of one thing led to progress elsewhere. Take the Industrial Revolution as an example. Initially people used goats or oxen on treadmills to power their tools. Later they were able to use the steam engine for power. This change gave people an overabundance of energy with which to power their tools. At first people used the same old machines to produce the same old stuff. Steam allowed people to work the machines longer and harder, which led to more abundance, which eventually led to new tools that produced new products and then the cycle took off.

Similarly, civilization—be it in Mesopotamia, Egypt, or China—did not develop until there was an overabundance of food from agriculture such that people could afford to specialize. Specialization allowed people to become masters at producing one thing *(aretê)* and then trade that one thing for all the other things they needed (comparative advantage). Everybody benefited. And that is the answer to the small-domain specialization (underkill) criticism. You must overdetermine the effects you seek and do so with an overabundance of causality (heterogeneous redundancy). You can afford to do so through the resource-saving tactic of specialization. In other words, when you look at the bigger picture, the balance between over- and underkill is the geodesic between your goals and your results. It is the most elegant way to solve the problem, and thus pleases Occam.

Similar logic explains why four causes are more elegant than one. The landscape of causing a contribution is so complex that the rate-limiting factor (the weakest link) of contributing is *clarity of thought.* When it comes to taking action, it is easier to think clearly with four causes than with one.

Truth

Is this theory of action true? It is *not* true that the four causes exist in the world in the same way that billiard balls do, but the theory does not claim to *describe* the world. It is a tool for thinking about the world. In this sense, the fact that it does not represent the world should not be held against it. To see why this is so, think about how people define *truth*.

People often say that a statement is true if and only if there is a one-to-one correspondence between the statement and reality. "The cat is on the mat" is a true statement if you can show that there exists a *felis catus* that is currently supported by a piece of coarse fabric. Under many common circumstances, however, this kind of truth may not exist. For example, the mathematician Benoit Mandelbrot asked a deceptively simple question: how long is the coast of Britain? The answer depends on how you measure it. You get a much shorter distance if you fly from one end to the other than if you drive a road that follows the island's contours. The road gives a shorter answer than if you walk the edge of the coast. An inchworm that worked its way around every rock on every beach would travel yet a longer distance. In short, as your measuring rod becomes shorter, the coastline becomes longer and there can be no truthful answer to the question: how long is the coast of Britain?

This observation suggests that people's intuitive definition of truth may not necessarily take them where they want to go. That is, an idea may be true but useless, or untrue and useful. Five examples show how this can be the case:

1. Whose love has had a greater effect on the world—the true love of some real but obscure farmers married for fifty years or Romeo and Juliet's fictional love? Whose love has inspired more love? Measured by the effect on others, whose love is more real, the real love or the fictional love?
2. A broken clock is accurate twice a day, as when the

clock says it is 1:05 and it is, in fact, 1:05. Although at 1:05 when this clock is *true* (in that there is a one-to-one correspondence between the broken clock and everybody else's clocks), this clock is useless. On the other hand, a clock that is reliably fast or slow—by minutes or hours—is useful. All you have to do is know how much to add or subtract to what's on the clock to get the correct time.

3. Some of the most important statements in life have an ambiguous relationship with truth. Searle pointed out that there are statements called performatives, such as, "With this ring I thee wed," or "I give you this," that weren't true before you say them, but become true by virtue of your having said them. The use of language in such a case is not to describe an event, but to make it happen.

4. There are nontruths with remarkable characteristics. These statements aren't true when they are said, but become true by virtue of having been said and acted upon. Searle argued, "One of the most remarkable capacities of the human mind is its ability to construct an objective reality of entities that in some sense exist only because we believe them to exist. I am thinking of such things as money, property, marriage, governments, and above all, language."

5. A related category of statements aren't true when said for the first time, but become true in time. The most striking of these include Newton's laws of motion that ignore friction, and the Declaration of Independence's, "We hold these truths to be self evident...." Friction is a dominant feature of matter, and it was anything but self-evident that people have inalienable rights. But today, when people have gone to frictionless outer space and have built nations on such unobvious self-evident truths, these untruths show their truth-value.

This observation is why playwright Eugène-Marin

Labiche concluded, "There are times when lying is the most sacred of duties." How so? Goethe believed, "For a man to achieve all that is demanded of him, he must regard himself as greater than he is." The truth is that you may not be up to the task of making a lasting contribution to the world, unless you lie to yourself and convince yourself that you are, in fact, capable of it. Step one is to stand fast (in Oprah's shoes) in the faith that you can make a lasting contribution. Step two is to constitute the lie to turn it into a truth.

These stories we tell ourselves (*I think I can, I think I can*) may not have a one-to-one correspondence with reality (because you wouldn't say it if you *really* thought you could). *Truth,* however, has two other definitions: that which independent observers agree upon and that which has a measurable effect. Because many people agree on what he does, and because he has a measurable effect on the world, this means that, yes, Virginia, there *really* is a Santa Claus, not in the ontological sense (the way bricks exist) but in the functional sense (the way numbers exist). It also means that some fictional figures have had more influence on real people than many real people have and therefore the fictional figures have greater functional existence. Consequently, what matters may not be the truth-value of ideas, but the *meaning* of them, because meaning is where the action is. For example, step into this house:

The small house says it's the most they can afford. The mess of toys speaks to lives out of control. The Spartan furnishings tell the story of just making it. The clothes on the clothesline mutter working poor. The stench of garlic shouts low class.

Or,

The size of the house says financial prudence. The toys on the floor proclaim that it's a child-centered family. The openness of the living room declares that they value not things, but people. The clothes on the line smile comfort and lack of pretension. The scent of garlic invites that they know how to cook and that they eat well.

Both paragraphs describe the same facts, the same truth. The house is the same, but that is not what matters. What matters is the interpretation, and that is the important difference between the two paragraphs. In other words, as literary scholar Erich Heller warned, "Be careful how you interpret the world: It is like that." The idea that texts or facts speak for themselves—interpret me no interpretations—is weapons-grade stupidity.

So? Gadamer argued that you understand something when you can apply it to your present situation. In other words, you understand it by putting it to use. The bottom line, to stay within the accounting metaphor, is William James' concept of the *cash value* of a theory. The cash value of the differing interpretations of the house lies, among other places, in that one interpretation leads a salesperson to pass the house by while the other interpretation leads to the potential sale of toys, prudent investment opportunities, and good food. The concept of *cash value* provides a way to answer the question: how long is the coast of Britain? The way is to ask: Why do you ask? If you want to fly it, the best answer is one length. If you want to drive it, the best answer is another length. If you want to walk it, the best answer is yet another length. In short, you measure the cash value of a theory with its practical consequences.

Realism

One reason to believe that you can make a lasting contribution has to do with the way in which a small change can make a big difference. Peter Senge said, "Small changes can produce big results—but the areas of highest leverage are often the least obvious." How does this work? Think of marginal analysis, how a small difference in one variable can make a big difference in another variable:

- In many Olympic races, the difference between winning and losing is measured in hundredths of a second, but this infinitesimal difference makes a huge difference in the lives of the competitors.
- A small change in the key lending rate can mean the difference of billions of dollars in the stock market.
- The space shuttle orbits the earth at 17,300 mph. To reenter the earth's atmosphere, it slows down to 17,125 mph, a difference of 1 percent.
- One person's DNA differs from another's by 0.0003 percent, yet Brian dies of a disease to which Gale is immune.

In other words, you achieve something that matters by giving rigorous meaning to the infinitesimal contribution that you can make. Your contribution may truly be infinitesimal, but that can be enough. Civilization has pivoted on the infinitesimal before. The infinitesimal is the fundamental trick of calculus, an indispensable step in the Scientific Revolution. Jacob Bronowski explained, "In [calculus], mathematics becomes a dynamic mode of thought, and that is a major mental step in the ascent of man. The technical concept that makes it work is, oddly enough, the concept of an infinitesimal step; and the intellectual breakthrough came in giving a rigorous meaning to that."

Failure

Nevertheless, isn't it possible that you will fail in your effort to make a lasting contribution? Of course. Contributing *is* difficult. But failure can be a necessary condition for greater success, as the following three examples show.

- Beethoven's deafness prevented him from playing the piano as an outlet for his talent so he rerouted his musical *aretê* to composing, and in so doing made a contribution that has lasted far longer than did the pleasure of those who heard him play.
- The fourteenth century witnessed the Black Death, which, for sure, was no party, but which weakened medieval theocracy enough to allow for the beginning of humanism and the Renaissance—the end of the Middle Ages and the beginning of the path to modernity.
- Had Vincent van Gogh succeeded in his ambition to be a clergyman, he would not have turned to painting and art itself would be the poorer.

Failure may be the *only* path to greater success. Remember that the next time the Demon of Defeat pops you in the nose.

Genius

But don't you have to be a genius to make a lasting contribution? Bronowski thought, "The Ascent of Man... is made by people who have two qualities: integrity, and at least a little genius." Kenneth Clark recognized, "In studying the history of civilisation one must try to keep a balance between individual genius and the moral or spiritual condition of a society. However irrational it may seem, I believe in genius. I believe that almost everything of value which has happened in the world has been due to individuals." So it would seem that genius is required; but William James maintained, "Genius, in truth, means little more than the faculty of perceiving in an unhabitual way." Moreover, Clausewitz held that "the field of genius...*raises itself above rules.*"

Such unhabitual perception and rising above the rules constitutes the essence of striving for *aretê*. People like you and me do not achieve this through mental power, but through knowledge, practice, and perception. Theodore H. White, for example, started with the perception that people live in idea boxes. He called the people who invented the boxes—Peel, Mitchell, Goddard—*power brokers*, thus giving the world a new way to think about politics. In so doing, White created an idea box of his own that people seek to live in. People now consciously strive to become power brokers. In this sense, White became a power broker, all of which started with the perception that "Most ordinary people lived their lives in boxes...."

Another example of attainable genius is that people could have made gliders hundreds of years earlier than they did, except that inventors, such as Leonardo da Vinci, were obsessed with the flapping wings of birds. Once people separated lift (the wing) from propulsion (the engine), they made rapid progress in airplane technology. In this sense, the airplane was what's called a "postmature discovery." Where did the breakthrough come from? Johann Bernoulli worked out the mathematics in 1738. If the development of the airplane was a function of Newton-like genius, humanity should have had airplanes soon after. It was not until 1799 that George Cayley successfully built a glider that could carry a person (some unsung ten-year-old boy). It took another eighty-five years until someone came up with a usable wing. According to John Anderson's *Introduction to Flight,* in 1884 Horatio Phillips made this contribution by experimenting with "every conceivable form and combination of forms" in a wind tunnel.

Surprisingly, even some big pure-science breakthroughs are the result of the kind of genius that you and I (can) have. Earth scientist Robert Hazen observed, "Watson and Crick's brilliant deduction [of the structure of DNA] was arrived at more by inspired guesswork and tinkering with models than by any step-by-step logic." The point is that Watson and Crick contributed by breaking the known rules of the day—not with genius of mind but with persistence of hand. They did so by tinkering and by knowing everything there was to know about the domain—and then learning one more thing. Bronowski grasped, "The hand is more important than the eye." This kind of genius is within the reach of each of us. In their book *The Social Life of Information,* John Seely Brown and Paul Duguid provided an example:

> There's a story told of a typesetter working on a Greek text at the Oxford University Press who announced he'd found a mistake in the text. As the typesetter couldn't read Greek, his colleagues and then his superiors dismissed the claim. But the man insisted. So finally an editor came down to the compositing room. At first, she, too, dismissed the idea, but checking more closely, she found there was an error. Asked how he knew, the typesetter said he had been hand-picking letters for Greek texts for most of his professional life and was sure that he'd never made the physical move to pick the two letters in that order before.

In short, we can all tinker with our work until we get it right. Contributing, like intelligence itself, is less about what you've got than how you use what you've got.

Summary

The four-cause theory of action does not describe the world. It is a tool that facilitates action. In this context, the final cause and the theory's potential inelegance are not a problem. Moreover, it is realistic to say that individuals can make lasting contributions, even if they fail along the way and even if genius is required of them. Think again of Nurse Bryan. She made use of constitutive rules in that her actions led to what became known as "Nurse Bryan's Rule." She gave rigorous meaning to the infinitesimal contribution that she could make. She made a lasting contribution, because she imposed a function (meaning) on an object (her actions) and began to use her actions as the institution of patient care. The theory of action also helps us to see her genius. It shows how a "not particularly distinguished" nurse "still made demands on people who in terms of training and position were her superiors." In short, the theory of action fits with other theories so you can have confidence in it as a tool to help you make a lasting contribution. But why should you try to contribute?

VIII

Why?

More people are killed out of righteous stupidity than out of wickedness.

—KARL POPPER

Given that it can be a blistering amount of work and that you might fail anyway, why would you want to try to make a lasting contribution to the world? I believe that contributing to the world is a worthy goal on its own, that making a contribution is a self-evident good, but I also know that not everybody shares my beliefs. So, the question remains: Why bother? Because both the results and process of making the effort are valuable.

Results

If you try to make a lasting contribution to the world, then you can achieve results that make the endeavor worth the effort, such as *sasuga*—the Japanese belief that if you are a master of one thing, then you are a master of all things. Other important results that can follow from the pursuit of contributing include learning the value of doubt and achieving a different way to look at ethics.

Doubt

Seeking *aretê* is part of trying to make a lasting contribution. *Aretê* is worth achieving, because as you seek to know all there is to know about a domain, you learn about the limits of knowledge. Bronowski observed, "The world is not a fixed, solid array of objects out there, for it cannot be fully separated from our perception of it. It shifts under our gaze, it interacts with us, and the knowledge that it yields has to be interpreted by us. There is no way of exchanging information that does not demand an act of judgment."

Our minds are open dynamic systems of knowledge in which everything can potentially interact with everything else in a multitude of ways. You must either assimilate each new piece of information into your existing structure of knowledge or change your existing structure of knowledge to the new information. If you don't, you won't make the information part of your system of knowledge. But this process is like herding Cheshire cats for at least six reasons:

1. When people think about something, they can only think about aspects or features of the thing. What is a brick? A building block, a paperweight, a weapon, an (I kid you not) ancient Chinese pillow, a metaphor. Also, the future can change the past. People once thought that bricks were strong materials with which to build. Given what engineers now know about earthquakes, bricks are not considered all that strong.

2. What people assume to be important determines what counts as knowledge. Historian Yoko Miyamoto demonstrated that Martin Luther identified the Turks as the devil's henchmen not because he had observed them to be devilish or henchman-like. Even if Luther had observed the Turks, this would not have counted as knowledge, because for Medieval Christians only the Bible could lead to

truth. The question, "Who are the Turks?" could only have an answer that came from the Bible so Luther drew "data" from the Bible that matched his prejudice for non-Christians.

3. Facts are a function of the systems of thought in which they occur, as Harvard educator William Perry explained in his essay, "Examsmanship and the Liberal Arts." Perry scrutinized the *fact* that Columbus discovered America:

> By whose calendar is it proper to say that Columbus discovered America in 1492? How, when and by whom was the year 1 established in this calendar? What of other calendars? In view of the evidence of Leif Ericsson's previous visit (and the American Indians), what historical ethnocentrism is suggested by the use of the word "discover" in this sentence? As for Leif Ericson, in accord with what assumptions do *you* order the evidence?
>
> These questions and their answers are not "more" knowledge. They are devastation. I do not need to elaborate upon the epistemology, or rather epistemologies, they imply. A *fact* has become at last "an observation or an operation performed in a frame of reference." A liberal education is founded in an awareness of frame of reference even in the most immediate and empirical examination of data. Its acquirement involves relinquishing hope of absolutes and of the protection they afford against doubt.... It demands an ever widening sophistication about systems of thought and observation. It leads,

Tad Waddington

not away from, but through the arts of games-manship to a new trust.

This trust is in the value and integrity of systems, their varied character, and the way their apparently incompatible metaphors enlighten, from complementary facets, the particulars of human experience.

4. People's ideas may not be as robust as they believe. For example, I'd bet that most people have little reason to doubt the *Oxford English Dictionary's* definition of the word *crusade*: "A military expedition undertaken by the Christians of Europe in the 11th, 12th, and 13th centuries to recover the Holy Land from the Muslims." Now use the same dictionary to look up some of the key words of this definition. The word *expedition* was not used in English until 1464; *undertaken* 1440; *military* 1585; and—get this—*Europe* 1957. If *Europe* in some sense did not exist until 1957, how could it have been crusading 700 years earlier?

5. The best course of action may be counterintuitive. For example, pilots learn to doubt their intuitions and to trust their instruments. In a cloud, you may feel that you are flying straight and even. Then you look at your instruments and see that you are spiraling down. If you continue to trust your intuition, you will crash.

6. I have seen great scholars cautiously and hesitantly apply techniques that *they invented*. It is, they say, too easy to make a mistake; you can't trust your gut, but you can trust systematic clear thought. I've seen businesspeople who were initially excited about a deal override their excitement and turn the deal down, because the numbers just didn't add up.

Bronowski summarized the importance of doubting what you know: "There is no absolute knowledge. And those who claim it, whether they are scientists or dogmatists, open the door to tragedy. All information is imperfect. We have to treat it with humility. That is the human condition." To fail to treat information with humility, continued Bronowski, led to "the concentration camp and crematorium at Auschwitz. This is where people were turned into numbers. Into this pond were flushed the ashes of some four million people. And that was not done by gas. It was done by arrogance. It was done by dogma. It was done by ignorance. When people believe that they have absolute knowledge, with no test in reality, this is how they behave."

In sum, to strive for *aretê* is an important part of trying to make a lasting contribution. In striving for *aretê* you learn how little you can know for certain, and this is a lesson worth learning. Mexican novelist Carlos Fuentes summarized, "In the name of certainty, the greatest crimes have been committed against humanity."

Ethics

If you try to make a lasting contribution, you can achieve a more sophisticated understanding of ethics. Many people believe that rules, such as the Ten Commandments, are the essence of ethics. But rules cannot be the essence of ethics, because Kurt Gödel's incompleteness theorem proved that there are truths that cannot be reached by the rules of the system. In other words, a statement can be true, but cannot be proved to be true. Proof is weaker than truth. This means that it is possible to make an ethical choice that cannot be supported by the rules of ethics. The philosopher Alasdair MacIntyre noted: "Such choice demands judgment and the exercise of the virtues requires therefore a capacity to judge and to do the right thing in the right place at the right time in the right way. The exercise of judgment is not a routinisable application of rules."

If George Bernard Shaw is right that, "The golden rule is that there are no golden rules," then what is the essence of ethics? Results. Striving for *aretê* and engaging in systems thinking help to give you the ability to think through the consequences of your decisions. The efficient cause involves taking seriously the results of your actions. It is nonsense to say, "I will do the right thing regardless of the consequences," because the consequences are part of the definition of *doing the right thing.*

Two examples help to clarify the difference between rule-adherence and judgment. The first concerns the Ford Pinto, which gained a reputation as "the barbecue that seats four," because when the Pinto was rear-ended, the gas tank often slammed into bolts sticking out of the differential. The bolts could then puncture the gas tank, resulting in a fire hazard. According to Mark Dowie, who first reported in *Mother Jones* magazine the Pinto problem, Ford could have prevented this design problem with a piece of plastic that weighed a pound and cost a dollar, but Lee Iacocca strictly enforced the rule of 2,000: the Pinto was not to weigh more than 2,000 pounds or cost more than $2,000. The life-saving piece of plastic would have broken the rules and put the car over the 2,000-pound and $2,000 mark. Hindsight—and the millions of dollars Ford lost in lawsuits—show that in the Pinto's case judgment should have trumped the rules.

The second involves imagining a scenario in which if you were to bear false witness, you would save a roomful of innocent people from certain death. There is a rule against bearing false witness, but there is no rule against inaction, so if you foolishly follow the rules, innocent people will die. This isn't a question of right or wrong. It is wrong to lie and wrong to allow innocent people to die. The question is, given the circumstances, which is the better choice? Under these conditions, I believe the lie is excusable.

The more general point is that because the world is ever changing, our ethics must also be adaptable. It is naive to believe that uncritically following a handful of simple rules always leads to good outcomes. This leads to the ethical insights of the existentialist philosophers Jean-Paul Sartre and Martin Heidegger. Human freedom entails responsibility, and as such, people are the uncontestable authors of their actions. This authorship comes from your authentic self. The reason you do not steal is not because there is a rule against it. You don't steal, because you are not a thief. You don't kill, because you are not a murderer. Ethics begins with who you are, what you value, and how you exercise your freedom to choose your reactions and, more important, your actions.

This view of ethics differs from the traditional view by *requiring* action. Take the Ten Commandments as an example. Only "observe the Sabbath" and "honor thy father and mother" require you to act. The rest—do not kill, commit adultery, take the Lord's name in vain, and so on—are all passive, as if good could come from simply not doing evil. But if you do not plant a crop, it will not grow spontaneously. The absence of evil does not guarantee good. Only causing good guarantees good. Ethics and action are inseparable.

Process

Often, however, worthy ends justify questionable means; so you should also question the process of trying to contribute. I mean by *process* what British classical scholar Gilbert Murray believed: "The things that we have called eternal, the things of the spirit and the imagination, always seem to lie more in a process than in a result, and can only be reached and enjoyed by somehow going through the process again. If the value of a particular walk lies in the scenery, you do not get that value by taking a short cut or using a fast motor-car." An important part of the process of trying to contribute is that it creates meaning in your life.

Meaning

Austrian psychiatrist Viktor Frankl, who survived the concentration camps at both Auschwitz and Dachau, explained where meaning comes from: "Everything can be taken from a man but one thing: the last of human freedoms—to choose one's attitude in any given set of circumstances, to choose one's own way." In *Man's Search for Meaning*, he observed that, "It is impossible to define the meaning of life in a general way. Questions about the meaning of life can never be answered by sweeping statements." He continued,

The meaning of life differs from man to man, from day to day and from hour to hour. What matters, therefore, is not the meaning of life in general but rather the specific meaning of a person's life at a given moment. To put the question in general terms would be comparable to the question posed to a chess champion: "Tell me, Master, what is the best move in the world?" There simply is no such thing as the best or even a good move apart from a particular situation in a game and the particular personality of one's opponent. The same holds for human existence.

This view means that you hold the power of interpretation, a power not to be underestimated. Where others see wheels within wheels, you see ball bearings. Where they see laziness, you see a chrysalis. Where they see a fury, you see a muse. Where they see a dog, you see a Buda dog-market, an opportunity. The philosopher Immanuel Kant believed that our minds constitute the world by imposing space, time, and causality; in the same way, our inherent power to interpret the world builds the possibility of meaning—and thus hope—into the structure of what it is to be human. There is always the possibility of grasping yet a bigger picture that makes sense of—gives meaning to—the current situation, however bleak it may be. No matter how much is taken, enough abides.

Meaning relates to the final cause through what Frankl called *attitudinal heroism,* the essence of which lies in your ability to choose your reactions to what happens to you in life. Meaning lies in how you exercise that choice. Philosopher Hannah Arendt wrote that this is "an act of existential choice unconstrained by principles or norms." For example, related Frankl:

> Once, an elderly general practitioner consulted me because of his severe depression. He could not overcome the loss of his wife who had died two years before and whom he had loved above all else. Now, how could I help him? What should I tell him? Well, I refrained from telling him anything but instead confronted him with the question, "What would have happened, Doctor, if you had died first, and your wife would have had to survive you? "Oh," he said, "for her this would have been terrible; how she would have suffered!" Whereupon I replied, "You see, Doctor, such a suffering has been spared her, and it was you who have spared her this suffering—to be sure, at the price that now you have to survive and mourn her." He said no word but shook my hand and calmly left my office. In some way, suffering ceases to be suffering at the moment it finds a meaning, such as the meaning of a sacrifice.

Meaning ties to how you make a contribution in another way. I oversimplified in Chapter One when I described the four causes. I wrote, "The final cause of a brick is to make a wall.... The final cause [of climbing a mountain]...is because it is there." But I also wrote, "Meaning lies in how you exercise...choice," and such choice is "unconstrained by principles or norms." The final cause of a brick isn't necessarily a wall; it is a paperweight, a weapon, a pillow, a metaphor—*you choose.* The final cause of mountain climbing may be exercise, because you want to stay healthy enough to know your grandchildren. Or it may be something completely different of your choosing. One can, to return to Frankl, "choose one's own way." Changing the final and formal causes, of course, alters the material and efficient causes as well. You prepare for and climb a mountain differently depending on why you want to climb it.

An old story shows how your ability to exercise unconstrained choice is the genesis of the final cause, and what a difference that can make. A traveler meets three bricklayers and asks each what he's doing. The first mutters, "Working for a buck." The second states, "Making a wall." The third proclaims, "Building a school that will educate children for generations." Each bricklayer is doing the same work, but the work of the third is imbued with more meaning than that of the other two.

Now hold on: in Chapter Four, when talking about Gadamer's hermeneutics and how you understand a text, I wrote that meaning arises as a dialectic between you and the text and that meaning is made manifest in application. In Chapter Five, I suggested that meaning lies in mythologizing your actions. In this chapter, I drew on Frankl to say that meaning has to do with unconstrained choice. Frankl also said that it was the people who had meaning, *who had something in the future to live for,* who survived the concentration camps. Moreover, in Chapter Four, when talking about lastingness, I said that meaning had to do with how consequences echo through time. So which is it?

I believe these different ways of looking at meaning point in the same direction, but each one emphasizes different aspects. Taken together, they resolve to the following: meaning arises (hermeneutics) from how you consciously (mythologize) interact (dialectic) with the world such that you seek to ethically (unconstrained choice) make a contribution (a values-based effect on the world) that lasts (future orientation). In short, meaning comes from mindfully trying to make a lasting contribution.

Summary

Trying to make a lasting contribution is worth the effort, because it can teach you the value of doubt, help you to take ethical action, and give more meaning to your life. In short, it makes you a better person. But what is a contribution?

IX

Contribution

Great thoughts reduced to practice become
great acts.

—WILLIAM HAZLITT

Up to now, I've focused on how to cause a lasting contribution, and why. The question remains: what is a
contribution? In Chapter Seven, I wrote that it isn't the
world that matters so much as how we think about it. In
Chapter Eight, I wrote that facts are a function of our
frame of reference and of the system of assumptions in
which they occur. But in Chapter Three, I wrote that
both the world and the mind are open dynamic systems. I have, however, not written enough about "inner"
and "outer." Inner has to do with the final and material causes—what you value and what you can do well.
Outer has to do with the formal and efficient causes—
navigating the world and getting results in it. Should
you approach making a contribution from the inside
out (here are my values; I'll seek to change the world to
fit my vision, such as by bringing beauty into the world)
or the outside in (there is a problem that needs solving;
I'll see if I can help)?

Recall in the discussion of constitutive rules in Chapter Five how lower-level things count as higher-level

things. A ball through the hoop counts as points. More points at the end of the game count as victory. Victory counts as winning, which in a bet counts as money. Some misguided people even count money as a measure of success. From Chapter Four, recall also that information is a relationship. It isn't found in the medicine that a doctor gives a patient. It isn't found in whether the patient lives or dies. Information is found in the *relationship* between the medicine the doctor gives the patient and the patient's health. Recall too from Chapter Four the phenomena of emergent properties, how under the right conditions a couple of dollars' worth of minerals and a couple of cups of water can become an avalanche-and-tea-stain-causing squirrel. Finally, from Chapter Eight, recall that meaning arises from how you consciously interact with the world such that you ethically seek to make a contribution that lasts.

Given all of this, what is a contribution? A contribution arises (as an emergent property) through the interplay (or dialectic) of matching (formal cause) what you know (material cause) and love (final cause) to what the world is and needs (efficient cause). A contribution happens because you count actions as values (constitutive rules). A doctor giving a patient an injection is not simply a matter of sticking a needle in somebody's arm. It counts as taking care of the patient. A contribution happens because there is an ongoing relationship between the inner world of your values and the outer world of reality. Therefore, it doesn't matter if you work from the inside out or from the outside in, because the inner and outer must meet. Think of the business example again. The product-driven company needs customers to buy its innovative products. The market-driven company needs to come up with products that meet customers' needs. Products and markets must meet.

The weasel word in the definition above is "arises." So I will be specific. To make a contribution that lasts, it is vital to have the four causes work together. This is similar to how Harvard business professor Michael Porter defined *strategy:* "Strategy is creating fit among a company's activities. The success of a strategy depends on doing many things well—not just a few—and integrating among them. If there is no fit among activities, there is no distinctive strategy and little sustainability." For example, in 1860 Sir Joseph Wilson Swan invented the light bulb. Thomas Edison, however, gets the credit, because he didn't just make a bulb. He provided lamps, wires, and a power station to light the bulbs. Together the four causes are more effective than any one of them alone. You can see this synergy more clearly by looking at examples of individuals who have made lasting contributions.

Jean Ann Lynch

Jean Ann Lynch observed that since unemployed poor people received some help from the government, it is the working poor who are most in need of help. Her final cause was to help. She understood that if people skimp on diapers, then their babies develop diaper rash, leading the babies to cry more and thus suffer an increased risk of child abuse. Her plan was to form an organization, called Baby Basics, to provide diapers to working-poor families. Her material cause was to ask for donations, all of which would go to diapers. Ultimately her efficient cause was a corollary of the Knickerbocker rule—apply diaper to ass.

Norman Borlaug

The political economist Thomas Malthus was not the only prominent thinker (only the most famous) to believe that humanity would face mass starvation as population outran the food needed to support it. These dire predictions failed to come true because they underestimated the role science would play in increasing food production. Called the Green Revolution, its Thomas Jefferson was the Nobel Prize-winning agricultural scientist Norman Borlaug. Borlaug's final cause entailed a tripling of Mexican wheat output and a 60 percent increase in wheat harvests in Pakistan and India. His material cause was a PhD in plant pathology. His formal cause was not that of most scholars of collecting academic butterflies. Instead it was the hard-nosed pursuit of pragmatic results. His efficient cause was to work on his crops all day every day, year after year.

Georgia Sadler

Malcolm Gladwell's book *The Tipping Point* describes Georgia Sadler's final cause as, "To increase the awareness of diabetes and breast cancer in the black community of San Diego." Her formal cause involved using hairstylists to spread awareness, because they have a captive audience and enjoy a trusting relationship with their clients. Her material cause was that "She wrote the material up in large print, and put it on laminated sheets that would survive the rough and tumble of a busy hair salon." On the front end, her efficient cause involved "[bringing] in a folklorist to help coach the stylists in how to present their information about breast cancer in a compelling manner." On the back end, "she set up an evaluation program to find out what was working and to see how successful she was in changing attitudes and getting women to have mammograms and diabetes tests, and what she found out was that her program worked."

John Harrison

For centuries the inability to navigate well at sea had cost thousands of sailors' lives. Calculating latitude, your distance north or south of the equator, was easy: use a sextant at noon to bring the sun's reflection to the horizon. This gives you two things—the ability to read your latitude off the markings on the sextant and a lot of one-eyed sailors who'd looked at the sun too often.

The problem of how to accurately determine longitude was not solved until the mid-1700s, some three hundred years after Columbus' voyage. Most of the people working on the problem favored the sexy solutions of using celestial events and complicated mathematics. The person who solved the problem was a self-taught clock-maker, John Harrison. His efficient cause was thirty-four years of painstaking tinkering on the material cause, which was a series of four clocks, called H1 to H4. A clock solves the problem because the earth turns 360 degrees in twenty-four hours. This means that every four minutes the sun appears to move one degree. If you know the time at a fixed point (such as Greenwich) and you know the time where you are, then every four minutes of difference between the two times means that you are one degree of longitude away from that fixed point. So there was a need to create a highly accurate clock that could withstand the hot-and-cold, rough-and-tumble, humid-and-arid life at sea.

The evolution of Harrison's clocks reveals his formal cause. His first attempt, H1, is seventy-two pounds and nearly a yard in every dimension. H2 and H3 are similar and, if anything, boxier. H4 is a dinner-plate-sized pocket watch. It has 4 percent of the weight and 0.001 percent of the volume of the other clocks, and is built on different principles. It is as if H1 were an elephant, H2 a hippopotamus, H3 a rhinoceros, and H4 a cheetah. In other words, Harrison embraced the PhD-like insight that the last step of the formal cause can be radically different from the previous steps.

Stetson Kennedy

Steven Levitt and Stephen Dubner's book *Freakonomics* tells the story of Stetson Kennedy, who made a lasting contribution by combating racism. His final cause was to break up the KKK. "Because Kennedy couldn't fight in World War II—he had had a bad back since childhood—he felt compelled to defend his country at home. Its worst enemy, he believed, was bigotry."

Stetson's material cause was "as any foolhardy, fearless, slightly daft anti-bigot would—to go undercover and join the Ku Klux Klan." His material cause was secret inside information.

His formal cause ran as follows: "What better way to defang a secret society than to infantilize—and make public—its most secret information?" So, "Wouldn't it be nice...to get the Klan's passwords and the rest of its secrets into the hands of kids all across the country?" His efficient cause involved asking Superman for help. "Kennedy thought of the ideal outlet for his mission: *The Adventures of Superman* radio show, broadcast each night at dinnertime to millions of listeners nationwide. He contacted the show's producers and asked if they would like to write some episodes about the Ku Klux Klan. The producers were enthusiastic. Superman had spent years fighting Hitler and Mussolini and Hirohito, but with the war over, he was in need of fresh villains. Kennedy began feeding his best information to the *Superman* producers." The result? "Instead of roping in millions of members as it had just a generation earlier, the Klan lost momentum and began to founder."

Lynne Cox

In 2002, Lynne Cox swam over a mile in the slushy waters of Antarctica. What in God's name possessed her to do that? That is, what was the final cause? She explained, "I just wanted to be great at something." The formal cause was extensive planning, including having her teeth sealed with fluoride so they wouldn't shatter in the cold. The material cause was thirty years of practice, including holding the world speed record for swimming the English Channel. The efficient cause was the will to keep swimming despite the breathtaking cold. What makes this odd act a lasting contribution? She did that which Kenneth Clark says civilization depends upon: she extended her powers of mind and spirit to the utmost and showed the world something of the nature of the heroic quality.

Summary

You can make a lasting contribution to the world if you pursue a worthy goal (final cause), master your resources (material cause), have a plan for maximizing your efficacy (formal cause), take sophisticated action (efficient cause), and coordinate the four causes so they work together.

The end

As a rule, at the *very end,* everybody dies. About this inevitability, Dylan Thomas advised, "Rage, rage against the dying of the light." But rage is only a final cause. The question is: how do you take effective action against the dying of the light? In Chapter Four, I wrote about *breaking rules.* You break the rules by changing the nature of the equation. Make it *as if* you would not die—vanished, but not gone—by having the best of you live on—echoing through time—through your lasting contribution.

Glossary

aretê   From Greek (αρετή); excellence of any kind.

Aristotle   384–322 BCE. Plato's student and Alexander the Great's teacher, Aristotle was a polymath who made important contributions to nearly every domain of study known at the time.

choice   The freedom that exists between stimulus and response.

considered action   Where "just do it" is action based on whack-a-mole epistemology—see a problem and bang it with a hammer—considered action is sophisticated action, based on taking multiple dimensions of a problem into consideration.

Dao   Also known by its older Romanization *Tao,* from the Chinese word 道, meaning *road, speech, to know,* and *Way,* as in *a sacred Way of being and conducting oneself.* For the Daoists, the Dao is found in nature. For the Confucians, the Dao enters society.

efficient cause   The action that makes a thing happen. A wood worker building a table is the efficient cause of the table.

empirical   Concerned with what is observable.

epistemology   Theory of knowledge. Epistemology asks the question: how do you know?

ethics   A system of values. Where economics is concerned with maximizing utility, ethics is concerned with maximizing goodness.

existentialism   A philosophical theory that focuses on the individual and how she uses her freedom and responsibility to constitute herself and create meaning.

final cause   The goal of a thing or action. The final cause of a table is to have a place where you can eat your meals.

formal cause   The idea (sometimes put into a plan or blueprint) of a thing or action. The formal cause of a table is the idea of or plan for the table: a flat surface, four legs, sturdy, so on.

geodesic   The shortest distance between two points. This path is not necessarily a straight line. They say that the shortest distance to a man's heart is through his stomach, surely a serpentine path.

hermeneutics Interpretation; making that which is difficult to understand easier to understand.

hermeneutic circle The problem that you can't understand a whole text unless you understand the parts of the text, and that you can't understand the parts of the text unless you understand their context, the whole text.

heterogeneous redundancy As used in this book, to generate causes of different natures that lead to the same desired outcome. For example, if you were hunting a submarine you would look (one method) for something big, listen (another method) for something mechanical sounding, and assess water temperature (yet another method) for an unnatural heat source. Taken together, these different approaches allow you to triangulate with greater certainty.

humanism A rational system of thought that gives primacy to human (rather than divine) matters.

information As used in its technical sense here, a relationship between sender and receiver resulting in decreased system randomness. Will the British attack by land or sea? The Colonists are uncertain; there is randomness in their system of thinking. Given that they have agreed, "One if by land and two if by sea," when they see one lantern, they are informed (less uncertain) as to the invasion route.

integrity From the Latin *integritās*. It has three aspects. First, integrity means complete or undivided; as in material, spiritual, or aesthetic wholeness; unity or oneness. It's what people refer to when they say, "Racial integration." Second, integrity means soundness, solidity, intactness, strength, an unbroken state. Think of "structural integrity." Third, integrity means an uncompromising adherence to a code of values: sincerity, candor, veracity, faithfulness, goodness, decency, conscientiousness, scrupulousness. It's what's meant by "moral integrity."

koan From Japanese (公案), a puzzle to ponder, the pondering of which can lead to understanding. Kurt Gödel developed the incompleteness theorem by using the statement, "This sentence is a lie" as a *koan*.

K-selection A reproductive strategy in which a species, such as the blue whale, has few offspring and invests a lot in each.

knowledge Information (in the nontechnical sense) that occurs at the intersection of empirical data and theory.

logos From Greek (λόγος), word, speech, argument, explanation, doctrine, principle, reason, plan. The root of *-ology*, as in *semiology* and *axiology* (a major focus of this book).

material cause The stuff that composes a thing or act, in the way that wood composes a table or the way practice composes *aretê*.

minimax A method for making decisions in which you seek to minimize the worst thing that could happen. For example, you might think that the worst thing that could happen is for you to have lived a meaningless life, so you decide to prevent this by striving to make a lasting contribution.

muga From Japanese (無我), a degree of mastery in which you can perfectly execute your thought.

myth A meaningful story.

ontology Concerned with the nature of being. Ontology asks the question: what is?

Platonic As used here, the idea that the world we see is but an imperfect copy of the world of pure, perfect, and unchanging essences. A table you can observe is but a shadow of the true, perfect essence of a Table.

r-selection A reproductive strategy in which a species, such as the termite, has many offspring and invests little in the success of any one of them.

rules A theory of how to do something. The *breaking of rules* is not to be confused with cheating, which is a violation of integrity.

sasuga From Japanese (流石), the notion that if you are a master of one thing, you are a master of all things. It is not true that expertise crosses domains or even that excellence in one area makes you smarter in general, but it is true that the process of becoming great at something helps you to understand the nature of *aretê*. This understanding can help you to perceive *aretê* in others and act as a guide to achieving excellence in new domains.

system A whole composed of parts, wherein the absence of any one part may destroy the nature of the whole. Picture a wind-up clock as a system. You can remove very few parts before it ceases to work and thus ceases to be a clock.

theory A system of ideas that explains something by connecting empirical data to other data and ideas.

thought experiment Biologists perform experiments on fruit flies, because even though the results they get are not directly applicable to humans, they can still learn a lot and fruit flies are cheap. The thought experiment is the thinker's fruit fly.

Tad Waddington

Lasting Contribution *koans*

1. Think of the example in the book's second para-
    graph of installing a speed bump to make cars slow
    down so the children in the playground will be safer.
    Suppose local authorities told you that regulations
    did not allow them to install a speed bump. Should
    you secretly put it in yourself? More broadly, what
    do you think of the activist notion of ethics that the
    book advocates?

2. French author Anaïs Nin said, "I knew...that our
    concept of the hero was outdated, that the mod-
    ern hero was the one who would...struggle with
    his myths, who would know that he himself cre-
    ated them, who would enter the labyrinth and
    fight the monster...." What do you think about
    self-conscious mythmaking? Can a story you tell
    yourself about yourself be meaningful?

3. The extremely knowledgeable Albert Einstein said,
    "Imagination is more important than knowledge."
    Throughout this book, you are asked to "Imagine
    that..." and to "Suppose you..." What role does
    imagination play in ethics? In getting results? In
    a meaningful life?

4. The formal cause can be obvious, as with the ad-
    vice, "If you say to yourself, 'I shouldn't do this,'
    then *don't do it.*" But it can also be tricky, as with
    computer scientist Jim Horning's, "Good judgment
    comes from experience. Experience comes from
    bad judgment." Since conception leads percep-
    tion, it is important to cultivate your ability to see
    formal causes. Can you find other examples that go:

pachyderm, pachyderm, pachyderm, cheetah? What kinds of formal causes do you find most fascinating? Most useful? What do your answers reveal about how you perceive the world?

5. Do the four causes adequately embrace the two seemingly different worlds in which we live, of mind and body? Of passion and reason? Of thought and action? Does this book adequately balance what is (empiricism) with what can be (imagination)? The ancient with the modern? The East and the West? Art and science? Do you have a better approach?

6. Reflect on Viktor Frankl's answer to the question posed to a chess master, "Tell me, Master, what is the best move in the world?" What does this suggest about how you should use the ideas in this book?

7. Why does this book treat rules as, to quote the poet William Blake (out of context), "mind-forged manacles?" How do rules relate to boxes? To identities? To existentialism? To freedom?

8. Literary critic Harold Bloom said, "Falstaff and Hamlet are considerably livelier than many people I know." What do you think of the notion that something may not exist in the world the way a brick does, but that it may have a powerful functional existence?

9. Bertrand Russell was reasonably certain that, "The trouble with the world is that the stupid are cocksure and the intelligent are full of doubt." And the French philosopher Voltaire asserted, "Those who can make you believe absurdities can make you commit atrocities." Are they right?

10. The way this book approaches both ethics and knowledge is based on the idea that everything can potentially interact with everything else. In this sense, the view of ethics grows out of the view of knowledge. Is there a better approach?

11. Philosopher John Searle argued that "Intentionality

rises to the level of the background abilities." Has this book deepened your understanding of *competence*? Of *quality*? Has it changed how you think about *leadership*?

12. A theme that runs throughout this book is the power of interpretation. This thought relates to your ability to choose your reactions, which is, said philosopher Hannah Arendt, "an act of existential choice unconstrained by principles or norms." What does the power of interpretation imply about freedom? Does the text support the idea that *anything goes*? That you are free to interpret a trout as a zebra?

13. What do you learn if you take an idea, such as *constitute, heroic, vocabulary,* or even *Santa Claus* and follow it throughout the text? Given the hermeneutic circle, how do you think your understanding of the book would change if you read it again?

14. Supreme Court justice Oliver Wendell Holmes held that, "A word is not a crystal, transparent and unchanged; it is the skin of a living thought and may vary greatly in color and content according to the circumstances and time in which it is used." Similarly, this book suggests that things, such as bricks, are a function of the formal cause and, thus, of ideas. Does this help you to see solid objects as manifestations of thought? Should it? Is this a useful way to see the world?

15. The book draws on Confucius' idea of secular immortality. What do you think of this? Since you only get one shot at it, can you see the importance of foreknowledge, *K*-selection, and redundancy? What will be your lasting contribution?

Lasting Contribution

References

Anderson, J. 1978. *Introduction to Flight*. New York: McGraw-Hill.

Arendt, H. 1958. *The Human Condition*. Chicago: University of Chicago Press.

Aristotle, 1986. *The Physics: Books I–IV*. Translated by P. Wicksteed and F. Cornford. Boston: Harvard University Press.

Benedict, R. 1946. *The Chrysanthemum and the Sword: Patterns of Japanese Culture*. Boston: Houghton Mifflin Company.

Berger, P. and T. Luckmann. 1980. *The Social Construction of Reality: A Treatise in the Sociology of Knowledge*. New York: Irvington Publishers.

Bowen, W. and N. Rudenstine. 1992. *In Pursuit of the PhD*. Princeton, NJ: Princeton University Press.

Bradbury, R. 1990. *Zen in the Art of Writing*. Santa Barbara, CA: Capra Press.

Bronowski, J. 1974. *The Ascent of Man*. London: Little, Brown and Company.

Brown, J. and P. Duguid. 2002. *The Social Life of Information*. Boston: Harvard Business School Press.

Brunswik, E. 1956. *Perception and the Representative Design of Psychological Experiments*. Berkeley: University of California Press.

Chi, M., M. Farr, and R. Glaser. 1988. *The Nature of Expertise*. Hillsdale, NJ: Lawrence Erlbaum Associates.

Chuang Tzu. 1964. *The Chuang Tzu*. Translated by B. Watson. New York: Columbia University Press.

Clark, K. 1970. *Civilisation: A Personal View*. New York: Harper and Row.

Clausewitz, C. 1968. *On War*. Translated by F. Maude. Harmondsworth, UK: Penguin.

Collins, J. and J. Porras. 1994. *Built to Last: Successful Habits of Visionary Companies*. New York: Harper Business.

Confucius. 2000. *Confucius*. Translated by D. C. Lau. Hong Kong: The Chinese University Press.

de Bono, E. January 25, 1997. "Away with the Gang of Three." *The Guardian*. London.

Dörner, D. 1996. *The Logic of Failure: Why Things Go Wrong and*

What We Can Do to Make Them Right. Translated by R. Kimber and R. Kimber. New York: Metropolitan Books.

Dowie, M. 1977. September/October. "Pinto Madness." *Mother Jones*.

Drucker, P. 1967. *The Effective Executive*. New York: Harper Collins.

Drucker, P. 2005. "Managing Oneself." *Harvard Business Review On-Point*. Product number 8770, pp. 1–10.

Frankl, V. 1963. *Man's Search for Meaning: An Introduction to Logotherapy*. Boston: Beacon Press.

Gadamer, H. 2004. *Truth and Method*. Translation revised by J. Weinsheimer and D. Marshall. New York: Continuum.

Gladwell, M. 2000. *The Tipping Point: How Little Things Can Make a Big Difference*. London: Little, Brown and Company.

Goldenweiser, A. 1937. *Anthropology: An Introduction to Primitive Culture*. New York: F. S. Crofts and Company.

Gould, S. 2002. "The Median Isn't the Message." http://cancerguide.org/median_not_msg.html.

Hawkins, J. and S. Blakeslee. 2004. *On Intelligence*. New York: Times Books.

Hazen, R. 2002. "The Joy of Science." Produced by The Teaching Company. Chantilly, VA.

James, W. 1978. *The Writings of William James: A Comprehensive Edition*, Edited by J. McDermott. Chicago: University of Chicago Press.

Kelly, R. 1999. *How to Be a Star at Work*. New York: Three Rivers Press.

Kiyosaki, R. and S. Lechter. 2000. *Rich Dad, Poor Dad: What the Rich Teach Their Kids About Money—That the Poor and Middle Class Do Not!* New York: Warner Books.

Laudan, L. 1977. *Progress and Its Problems: Toward a Theory of Scientific Growth*. Berkeley: University of California Press.

Lévi-Strauss, C. 1955. "The Structural Study of Myth." In *Myth: A Symposium*. Edited by T. Soebeok. Bloomington: Indiana University Press.

Levitt, S. and S. Dubner. 2005. *Freakonomics: A Rogue Economist Explores the Hidden Side of Everything*. New York: Harper Collins.

Lin, Y. 1967. *The Chinese Theory of Art*. London: Heinemann.

Lowie, R. 1936. *Essays in Anthropology: Presented to A. L. Kroeber in Celebration of His Sixtieth Birthday, June 11, 1936*. Berkeley: University of California Press.

MacIntyre, A. 1984. *After Virtue: A Study in Moral Theory*. South Bend, IN: University of Notre Dame Press.

Mandelbrot, B. 1967. "How Long Is the Coast of Britain? Statistical Self-Similarity and Fractional Dimension." *Science.* Vol. 156, No. 3775. pp. 636–638.

McKee, R. 1997. *Story: Substance, Structure, Style and the Principles of Screenwriting.* New York: Harper Collins.

Miyamoto, Y. 1993. "The Influence of Medieval Prophecies on the Western Views of the Turks: Islam and Apocalypticism in the Sixteenth Century." *Journal of Turkish Studies:* 17: 125–145.

Moore, C. 2004. *In Other Words.* New York: Walker and Company.

Murray, G. 1921. *The Legacy of Greece.* Edited by R. Livingstone. Oxford: Clarendon Press.

Omori, S. and T. Katsujo. 1990. *Zen and the Art of Calligraphy: The Essence of Sho.* Translated by J. Stevens. New York: Penguin.

Oxford University Press. 1999. *The Oxford English dictionary on CD-ROM.* New York: Oxford University Press.

Perry, W. 2003. "Examsmanship and the Liberal Arts," in *The Norton Reader,* 4th ed., General Editor A. Eastman, 227–237. New York: W. W. Norton and Company.

Piper, W. 1976. *The Little Engine That Could.* New York: Platt and Munk.

Rhodes, R. 1995. *How to Write: Advice and Reflections.* New York: William Morrow and Company.

Russell, B. 1957. *Why I Am Not a Christian.* New York: Touchstone.

Saint-Exupéry, A. 2004. *The Little Prince.* London: Egmont Books.

Searle, J. 1983. *Intentionality: An Essay in the Philosophy of Mind.* Cambridge: Cambridge University Press.

Searle, J. 1995. *The Construction of Social Reality.* New York: Free Press.

Senge, P. 1990. *The Fifth Discipline: The Art and Practice of the Learning Organization.* New York: Doubleday/Currency.

Shannon, C. 1948. "A Mathematical Theory of Communication." *Bell System Technical Journal* 27: 379–43, 623–56.

Shen T. 1967. *The Chinese Theory of Art.* Edited by Lin Yutang. London: Heinemann.

Simon, H. 1983. *Reason in Human Affairs.* Palo Alto, CA: Stanford University Press.

Smith, J. 1993. *Map Is Not Territory: Studies in the History of Religions.* Chicago: University of Chicago Press.

Suzuki, D. 1970. *Essays in Zen Buddhism.* London: Rider.

Trump, D., R. Kiyosaki, M. McIver, and S. Lechter, S. 2006. *Why We Want You to be Rich: Two Men—One Message.* Rich Press.

von Neumann, J., and O. Morgenstern. 1944. *Theory of Games and Economic Behavior.* Princeton, NJ: Princeton University Press.

White, T. 1978. *In Search of History: A Personal Adventure.* New York: Harper Collins.

Winfrey, O. 2004. "Oprah Winfrey: Heart of the Matter." Biography. Arts & Entertainment Television Network.

Lasting Contribution

Index

About the Author

Tad Waddington (文達德) received his MA from the University of Chicago's Divinity School, where he focused on the history of Chinese religions. He earned his PhD from the University of Chicago, in measurement, evaluation, and statistical analysis. He is currently director of performance measurement for Accenture. His lasting contribution is a work in progress, but to date has involved rigorously demonstrating the tremendous value that companies can realize from training their employees, work for which he has won numerous awards. See *Return on Learning* (Agate, 2007), which he coauthored. He can be reached at tad@lastingcontribution.com, or visit www.lastingcontribution.com.